ULTIMATE KABUKI DROP RESOURCE

Includes 6 DIY Kabuki Drop Design Plans

J C Sum

Contributions by Darren Tien & Adeline Ng

National Library Board, Singapore Cataloguing-in-Publication Data

Name(s): Sum, J C, 1976- | Tien, Darren, author. | Ng, Adeline, author.
Title: Ultimate Kabuki Drop Resource : Includes 6 DIY Kabuki Drop Design Plans / J C Sum ; contributions by Darren Tien & Adeline Ng.
Description: Singapore : Concept : Magic, [2016] | Includes bibliographical references.
Identifier(s): OCN 962334583 | ISBN 978-981-11-1681-0 (paperback)
Subject(s): LCSH: Kabuki--Stage-setting and scenery--Handbooks, manuals, etc.
Classification: DDC 792.0952--dc23

© **Copyright 2016 by J C Sum.**

No part of this publication may be reproduced or transmitted in any form or by any means, electronic or mechanical, including photocopy, recording, or any information storage and retrieval system, now known or to be invented, without permission in writing.

Disclaimer

Fair Use of Photos. In several instances, photos from manufacturers' catalogues or websites have been used as examples of specific Kabuki Drop systems or to promote a particular design. Photo credits and links to the source material are given where applicable.

All Rights Reserved

The purchase of this book entitles only the book owner to build or have built any or all of the DIY Kabuki Drop systems contained therein for his/ her sole use. Any person borrowing the book or copying it illegally does not have this legal privilege.

All commercial manufacturing rights of any of the DIY Kabuki Drop systems contained in this publication are reserved and strictly remain the sole property of the author.

The author accepts no responsibility for damages or injuries resulting from the fabrication or performance of any of the DIY Kabuki Drop systems in this book.

In purchasing this book, you agree to these terms that will be enforced by international law.

CONTENTS

About the Author	6
Introduction	8
History of Kabuki Drop	11
Kabuki Stagecraft & Curtain Drop	13
Evolution of the Kabuki Drop	19
Basic Components of the Kabuki Drop	22
Manual Kabuki Drop Systems	34
Electronic Kabuki Drop Systems	42
Double Kabuki Drop System	54
Build, Buy or Rent Kabuki Drop Systems	57
Bibliography	66
DIY Kabuki Drop Systems	71
World's Easiest Curtain Drop	73
"The Peel" Drop	77
"The Pull" Drop	81
"Pins & Loops" Drop	84
"Pull Back" Drop	99
"Roll & Drop" Drop	108

ABOUT THE AUTHOR

Born & raised in Singapore, J C Sum is a headline entertainer, author & creative entrepreneur.

He is an international award-winning illusionist and has performed over 3500 shows in 34 countries on 4 continents. More than 120 million people have seen his magic on live shows & television with appearances on 26 programs across the world (www.jcsum.com).

J C is one of the most commercially successful illusionists in Asia and currently performs regularly as a headline entertainer for luxury cruise liners and corporate events in Asia, Europe and the Middle East.

As a creative entrepreneur, he runs a magic production house that produces shows and consults for events & TV. He also developed several successful online properties in niche domains such as IllusionBooks.com, IllusionBookStore.com and BackstageBusinessAcademy.com.

He has authored more than a dozen books covering a variety of subjects including technical illusion design, theatre stage craft as well as business & marketing for creatives.

J C graduated from the National University of Singapore with a Bachelors of Arts in English Language & Sociology with a minor in Philosophy. Since 2008, J C has given numerous talks locally & overseas on his perspective and approach to creativity and creative entrepreneurship for numerous organizations as well as TedX Talks and TechFests.

He has been nominated for a "Spirit of Enterprise" business award and has been featured in leading business publications such as The Business Times and The Edge.

J C is the curator of MagicKabukiDrop.com, the world's most comprehensive resource site on Kabuki Drops, a stagecraft technique and curtain release system.

He is also the inventor of the Pro Magic Kabuki Drop System which is a low-cost & lightweight manual Kabuki Drop system.

INTRODUCTION

A Kabuki Drop is a stagecraft technique and a release system that drops an open suspended curtain to the floor for a dramatic reveal.

It is often used in theatrical stage performances or special events to reveal a cast of performers, stage set or product.

A curtain or drape is suspended and held open by a specially designed system that holds the cloth securely until it is needed to be released.

The system is generally attached to some kind of overhanging horizontal support structure like a flying bar or lighting truss. The trigger mechanism to release the cloth can be activated either manually or electronically.

The modern-day Kabuki Drop finds its roots in the historic Japanese dance-drama, Kabuki Theatre. Traditionally, a curtain drop was used as a stagecraft technique to reveal a change of a scene. This technique was known as "Furiotoshi", which literally means, "shake down to reveal".

However, resource material has always been scarce and there is little information on the details of Kabuki Drop systems. In 2014, I decided to spearhead a project to put together the most comprehensive resource on the theatrical curtain drop system and together with a team, I put together the content in this book that explores the history, techniques, components, workings and systems of Kabuki Drops.

Thanks to Darren and Adeline for their invaluable work, time and effort on this project.

Besides being interested with the history and workings of Kabuki Drops, I have also been fascinated with the actual mechanisms and designs of Kabuki Drops, having worked with different systems at corporate events and launches over the years.

All the systems used some kind of electronic solenoid and one constant drawback was the systems were not 100% reliable. This is due to the fact that there are multiple points of possible failure ranging from solenoid mechanisms not working to voltage dropping and DMX reading errors. I was also surprised at how expensive Kabuki Drop systems were.

The unreliability of electronic systems is one reason why many theatre practitioners prefer manual systems.

While I've built a career designing illusions, my side pet project has been designing an inexpensive and 100% reliable Kabuki Drop system.

I've designed a professional manual system that I manufacture called the "Pro Magic Kabuki Drop System" but have also designed half a dozen DIY versions along the way. In fact, the very first drop I ever designed was back in 1996 when a friend asked me to design a "glitter" drop for a church function.

For the first time, I share my original DIY designs in this book. Each Kabuki Drop system includes measurements as well as detailed step-by-step instructions on what you need to get and how to put it together.

INTRODUCTION

Even if you do not have a production or technical background, you will be able to understand how to go about making each system through clear descriptions and drawings.

All designs can be made easily without a professional workshop or machining although you will need to cut, drill, saw and sew items that are readily available at good hardware stores.

In short, you can really "do it yourself"!

I wish you all the best and happy dropping!

J C Sum
Nov 2016

HISTORY OF KABUKI THEATRE

Kabuki is a classical Japanese dance-drama. It is often referred to as "the art of song and dance". The word Kabuki is derived from the Japanese verb 'Kabuku', meaning out of the ordinary or bizarre.

This is the reason why the stylization of drama and the elaborate make-up worn by the performers belong characteristically to the Kabuki Theatre.

The history of Kabuki extends for about 400 years, and it was pioneered during the Edo period, which is a period in Japanese history ranging between 1603 - 1868.

Its origin begun in Kyoto, where a shrine maiden, named Izumo no Okuni, would use the city's dry Kamo Riverbed as a stage to perform unusual dances for passersby.

These onlookers would soon find her daring parodies of Buddhist prayers both entertaining and mesmerizing. Soon, other troops began emulating her, and this became Japan's first dramatic performance form catered to the common people.

Slowly over the years, Kabuki evolved from street performances, to performances in theatre and teahouses.

By relying on heavily flamboyant makeup (or 'keshou'), and facial expressions instead of masks, and focusing on historical events and everyday life rather than folk tales, Kabuki set itself apart from the upper-class dance theater form called "Noh".

The unmistakable melodrama provided a unique commentary on society during the Edo period.

Till today, Kabuki still lives on as an integral part of Japan's rich cultural heritage, extending its influence beyond the stage, to television, film and anime.

KABUKI STAGECRAFT & CURTAIN DROP

KABUKI STAGECRAFT

The Kabuki theatre is well known for its use of various stage effects, due to its fondness for spectacle. Its distinctive features include peculiar stage designs, midair performances (or "Chunori"), and its unconventional use of curtains (or "Maku").

Traditional Kabuki Theatre
Photo Credit: Shibai Ukie by Masanobu Okumura (1686-1764)

KABUKI STAGECRAFT & CURTAIN DROP

Modern Kabuki Theatre
Photo Credit: Kanamaruza Theater (Japan Guide)

The characteristic feature of the Kabuki stage design includes the "hanamichi", a raised passageway leading from the left side of the stage, through the audience, to the back of the theatre (used to highlight entrances and exits of actors).

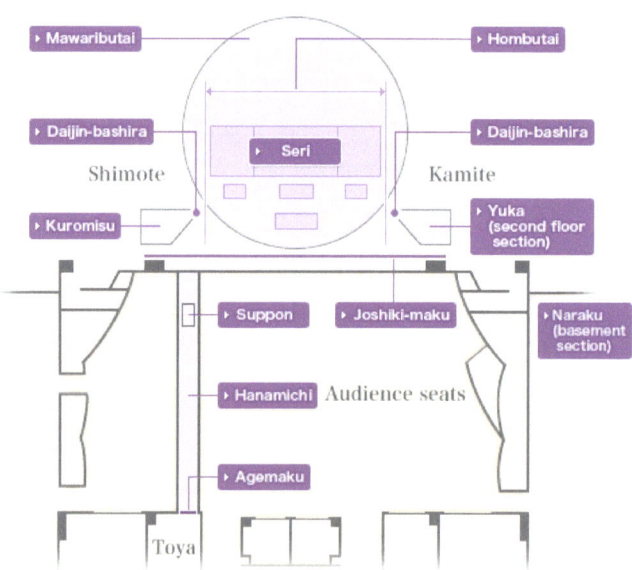

Kabuki Theatre Layout
Image Credit: Invitation to Kabuki, Japan Arts Council

Kabuki Theatre Trapdoor
Photo Credit: Jikabuki Project

Trap doors and lifts (or "seri") were incorporated in Kabuki, both for changes of scene and for surprise entrances and exits. The revolving stage (or "mawari butai"), is also sometimes used to produce a scenery-change effect, much akin to the fade-out and fade-in of film techniques.

TRADITIONAL KABUKI DROP

The use of curtains is a very important stagecraft technique used in Kabuki theatre.

Photo Credit: Kabuki-za Theatre

In traditional Kabuki theatre, special curtains, such as the "dandaramaku" (a large curtain with wide red and white horizontal stripes used as a temporary background), or more commonly the "asagimaku" (a pale blue curtain used for entrances), are used for the Kabuki drop to achieve different dramatic stage effects.

The "asagimaku" is often used, because its monotone, singular pale blue color can effectively juxtapose with the new scene's flamboyant colors, to amplify the transition.

There are various types of curtains being employed in a typical Kabuki theatre and each has distinct uses to create different theatrical and dramatic effects:

- Stage-set curtains (or "Dogumaku") are scenery curtains, where actual scenery such as mountain, waves, and wall are painted on.

- Mist curtains (or "Kasumimaku") are used to hide musicians on stage when they are not performing.

- Pale blue curtains (or "Asagimaku") are notably used for "Furiotoshi", which is the effect we now know as the "Kabuki Drop".

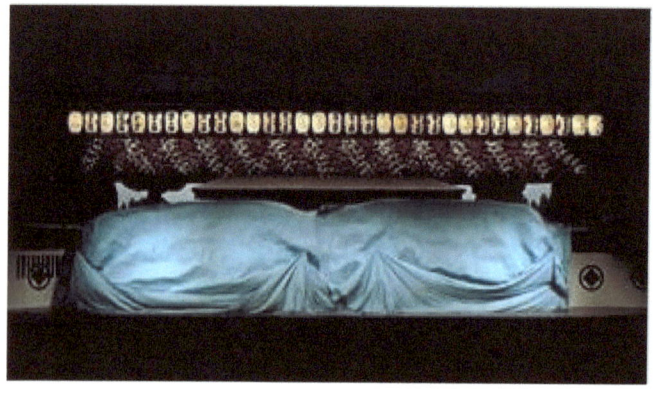

Traditional Kabuki Drop
Photo Credit: Invitation to Kabuki (Japan Arts Council)

"Furiotoshi" was first introduced to the Kabuki theatre in the late 18th century, as sophistication of the scenic effects on stage advanced steadily over the years.

"Furiotoshi" is the dramatic technique of making the stage instantly visible by dropping the curtain previously hung to conceal stage. Whisked down to the accompaniment of the clapping of the wooden "ki" (two wooden clappers), "Furiotoshi" allows for sudden scene changes, while "geza" music is used to maintain the audience's tension.

"FURIOTOSHI" = KABUKI DROP

The "Furiotoshi" was constructed using a "Furidake". A "Furidake" is simply a bamboo pole with small prongs or pegs attached to it at regular intervals. These pegs act as "drop points" for the Kabuki curtain (or "maku"). The pole is suspended, using rope over the stage, parallel to the stage front.

The pole is rotated and held in place so that the pegs point upwards. The curtain is hung on these pegs via curtain loops so that it covers the stage.

FRONT VIEW

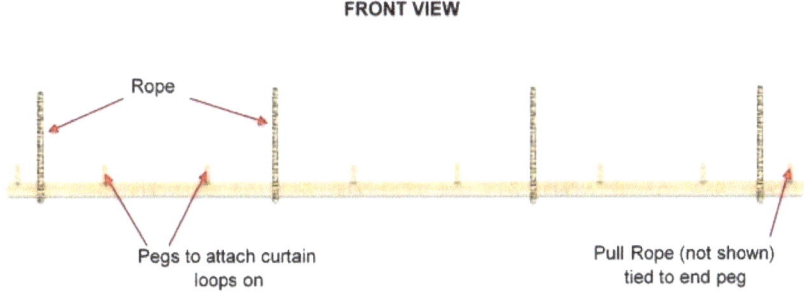

Image Credit: Magic Kabuki Drop

During the play, a rope attached to one of the end pegs is pulled by a "kurogo" (a 'black boy' or 'black clothing' stage assistant dressed and hooded in black). A "kurogo" goal is to be "invisible" and as inconspicuous as possible, who helps Kabuki actors, and carry out various stage duties.

This rotates the pole forward, resulting in the curtain loops slipping off the pegs and allowing the curtain to fall to the floor.

SIDE VIEW

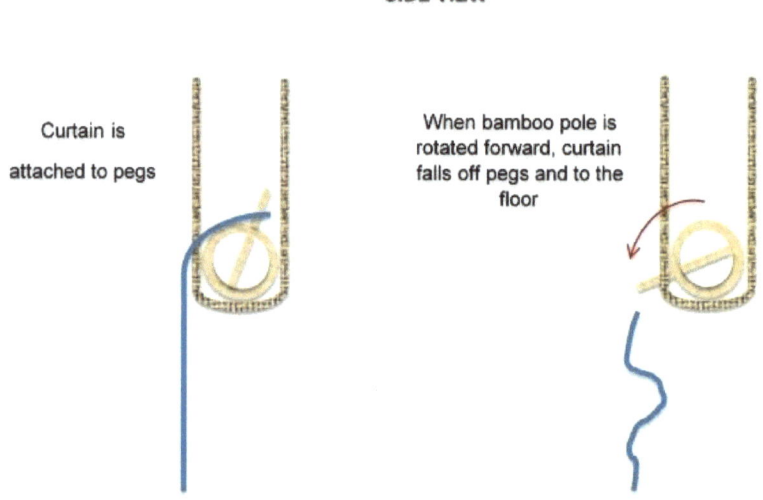

Image Credit: Magic Kabuki Drop

The "asagimaku" is thereafter swept away by stage assistants, and the effect is much like a quick cut in a movie, foreshadowing the taking place of a powerful scene.

Conversely, when the stage is visible and the curtain is dropped from the ceiling to instantly conceal the stage, the dramatic technique is called "Furikabuse" (shake down to conceal).

EVOLUTION OF THE KABUKI DROP

Traditionally, the Kabuki drop was used in the context of the historic Japanese dance-drama, Kabuki Theatre. It was formerly called "Furiotoshi", which literally means, "shake down to reveal".

Over the years, this technique has been retained in modern theatre to change a scene in an instant or to execute a theatrical reveal.

With its adoption in western theatre name, the "Furiotoshi" technique has since been simply referred to as the "Kabuki Drop" within the theatre and event industry.

MANUAL KABUKI DROP

The classical method of the curtain drop involved manual labor, where stage crew members released the curtain manually by way of a pull cord or using a pole that caused the curtain to drop to the floor.

Over time, there have been improvements to the manual curtain drop. There have been improvements in design and construction methods with modern materials, making it easier to build and be more reliable.

ELECTRONIC KABUKI DROP

Modern advancements in the curtain drop include the use of electronically powered magnetic systems called 'solenoids'. These electronic systems trigger the drop of the cloth electronically by activating a lever, spring-loaded pin or electro-magnet, depending on the specific design of the system.

PNEUMATIC KABUKI DROP

A variety of the modern Kabuki Drop is the Pneumatic Kabuki Drop. The Pneumatic Kabuki Drop system is an electro-mechanical system that uses compressed gas (from a pneumatic air tank) to trigger the drop. When triggered, a switch converts an electric current to air current. The air current activates a pneumatic cylinder with a pin, effecting the curtain drop.

In concept and methodology, a pneumatic system works almost identically to an electronic (linear solenoid) drop system.

This resource will not explore pneumatic systems but you can explore the following references.

- http://en.wikipedia.org/wiki/Pneumatic_cylinder
- http://www.pneumadyne.com/pneumatic-solenoid-valves.html
- http://www.stage-kinetik.de/en/pneumatic-systems.html

DOUBLE KABUKI DROP

One variation of the Kabuki Drop is the advent of the "Double Kabuki drop". The traditional drop is a SINGLE Drop. That means the curtain will already be opened up in place and covering the stage.

Activating the curtain drop will drop the curtain to the floor revealing what is on stage.

A DOUBLE kabuki drop means the curtain starts off rolled up and is held in place at the top of the stage proscenium (on the flying bars). Activating the curtain drop will open up the curtain so that it covers the stage. Activating the curtain drop a second time will drop the curtain to the floor revealing what is on stage.

A double drop can be activated either manually or electronically and ANY system can be adapted as a double drop.

BASIC COMPONENTS OF THE KABUKI DROP

There are four basic components of a Kabuki Drop system:

- Flying Bar
- Curtain
- Drop Points
- Trigger Mechanism

FLYING BAR

The flying bar is the horizontal support structure or bar that the Kabuki Drop system with curtain is hung from.

In a theatre, you would "fly" the Kabuki Drop system from the flying bars.

For events, you might use the rigging points in a venue or lighting truss that has been set up.

You could also use a makeshift horizontal support such as running a horizontal lighting truss or pole between two lighting stands.

Regardless of the flying bar used, it is important that the support is rated or endorsed to take the weight required for the Kabuki Drop.

CURTAIN

The perfect Kabuki fabric is one that is lightweight, durable and inherently flame retardant. IFR (inherently flame retardant) polyesters that can be sewn with minimal seams are the choice of the industry. Lightweight cloth is favored, to deliver a billowy effect.

Different fabric materials and thicknesses are used to create different effects for the Kabuki Drop. For example, opaque, translucent or transparent fabrics all create different visual effects under stage lighting, video projection and daylight.

Curtain Preparation

There are several ways to prepare the curtain for Kabuki Drops:

Option 1: Grommets

The most common way to prepare the curtain is to fit it grommets.

"A grommet is a ring or edge strip inserted into a hole through thin material, typically a sheet of textile fabric, sheet metal and or composite of carbon fiber, wood or honeycomb. Grommets are generally flared or collared on each side to keep them in place, and are often made of metal, plastic, or rubber.

They may be used to prevent tearing or abrasion of the pierced material or protection from abrasion of the insulation on the wire, cable, line being routed through the penetration, and to cover sharp edges of the piercing, or all of the above." Wikipedia.

Grommets used for Kabuki Drops are always made of metal.

BASIC COMPONENTS OF THE KABUKI DROP

To prepare to fit the grommets, first fold the edge of the cloth over to make a wide hem.

You can purchase a grommet kit from a general hardware store, haberdashery shop or curtain maker. Just follow the instructions that come with the kit to attach the grommets. Or, you can learn how to attach grommets to the curtain here.

Attach the grommets to either corner of the top of the curtain and the rest are spaced about 12" from each other, or wider depending on the number of drop points you intend to use.

Option 2: Header with Grommets

Instead of directly fitting the top edge of the curtain with grommets, a more sophisticated design is to make a header for the top of the cloth. The header runs the entire width of the cloth.

The header is made from 3" nylon webbing. The bottom 1" has a length of Velcro sewn onto the entire length of the header.

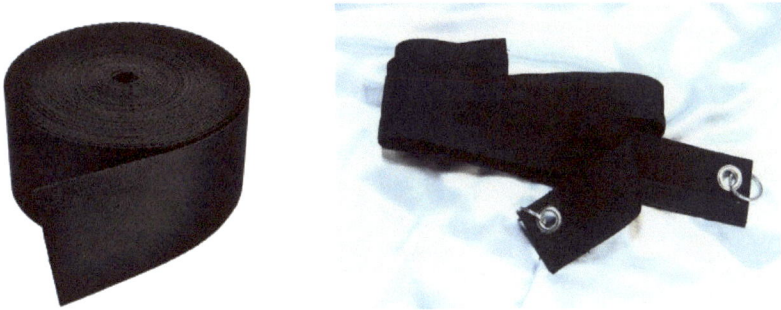

1" Grommets are attached to the top 2" of the header, evenly spaced apart.

With this method, a corresponding length of 1" Velcro is sewn across the entire top edge of the curtain. The curtain is attached to the header via the Velcro strips and the header is attached to the Kabuki drop point or mechanism.

BASIC COMPONENTS OF THE KABUKI DROP

Note:

In the traditional "rolling pole" method, the grommets are directly placed over the drop points ("pegs") to hold up the curtain.

However, in most Kabuki Drop systems that use grommets, an additional attachment is required to connect the curtain to the drop point system.

There are several hardware component options available:

Split Ring

This is a large steel key ring that is allows you slide a loop-shaped object onto it. Typically, a 1.5" stainless steel split ring is used for Kabuki Drops. This is slipped through the grommets and then attached the Kabuki drop point or mechanism.

Carabiner

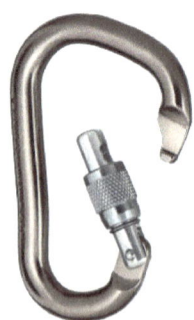

Also known as a Spring Hook, this piece of hardware is metal loop with a spring-loaded gate. This hooks you to "lock" the carabiner onto the grommet and also attaches to the Kabuki drop point or mechanism.

Shackle

Also known as a "gyve", this is a U-shaped piece of metal secured with a clevis pin or bolt across the opening, or a hinged metal loop secured with a quick-release locking pin mechanism.

The bolt of the shackle is threaded through the grommet and the shackle is "locked" into place. The U-shaped part is attached to the Kabuki drop point or mechanism.

Heavy-duty Cable Ties

Cable ties are an easy solution and are lightweight. Be sure to use cable ties that are at least 10mm wide to ensure they can hold the weight of the curtain.

BASIC COMPONENTS OF THE KABUKI DROP

Other Attachments

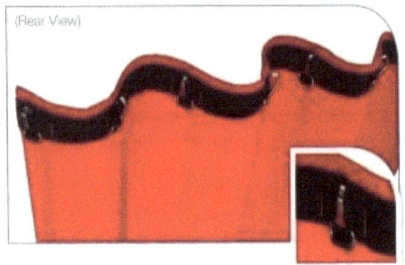

Tie Tapes

Tie Tapes are the most common top finish. Modacrylic tie tapes are 25mm wide by 400mm long sewn to each side of the 50mm modacrylic or polypropylene webbing. A coloured centre tie is standard.

Image Credit: J&C Joel

Check out a variety of other curtain attachments available from manufacturers such as J&C Joel.

Option 3: D-Rings with Velcro Straps

This method of preparing the curtain does use any grommets but uses Velcro instead.

A strip of hook-side 2" Velcro (the hard side) is sewn on each top edge of the curtain; i.e. one strip each on the front and back. The Velcro is sewn across the width of the curtain.

The attachment to connect the curtain to the drop point has to be custom made. Each attachments is made from a single 2"-wide strip of loop-side (the soft side) Velcro.

The reason for using the loop side of the Velcro is because this side wears out over time and needs to be replaced. It is much easier to replace when it is not sewn down onto the curtain.

This single strip of loop-side 2" Velcro (5" long) is looped through the straight end of a 2" D-Ring, folded over and sewn tightly together just under the D-Ring. This creates a "Velcro clip", where the two ends of the Velcro act as the tabs of the "clip".

FRONT VIEW

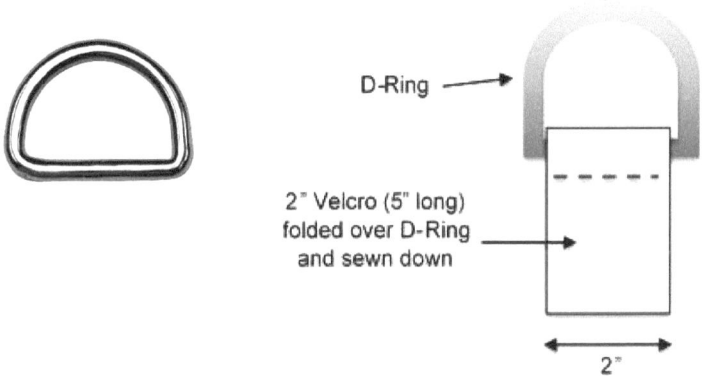

Image Credit: Magic Kabuki Drop

BASIC COMPONENTS OF THE KABUKI DROP

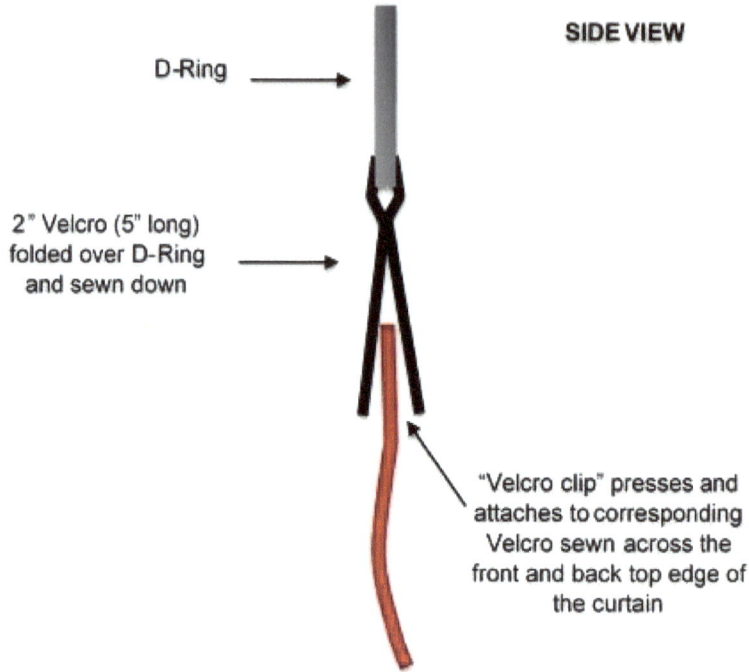

Image Credit: Magic Kabuki Drop

This allows the Velcro tabs to be "clipped" onto the top of the Kabuki curtain. The Velcro tabs attach to the corresponding Velcro strips sewn across the width of the curtain. (Think of the two flaps of Velcro on the D-Rings as breads and the top of the curtain as the filling – the curtain being sandwiched in the middle of the two flaps).

The D link is then attached to the Kabuki drop point or mechanism.

The use of Velcro allows for ease adjustments. This is so that there is flexibility in terms of shifting of the rigging points, assuming different set-ups for the Kabuki Drop is used for the same particular curtain.

Option 4: Curtain Clip or Clamp Attachments

Most Kabuki Drop systems, whether manual or electronic, require the curtain to be prepared with grommets, Velcro and/ or other attachments.

However, there are a few manufacturers that have developed fabric clamp accessories so that the curtain does not need any preparation or grommets.

This is especially useful if you are using a specific delicate fabric that you do not want to puncture holes in. The clamp system also allows for easy adjustment without the need to line up drop points and curtain attachments perfectly during set-up.

Manufacturers of these fabric clamps include Gerriets, Drape Kings and MagicFX.

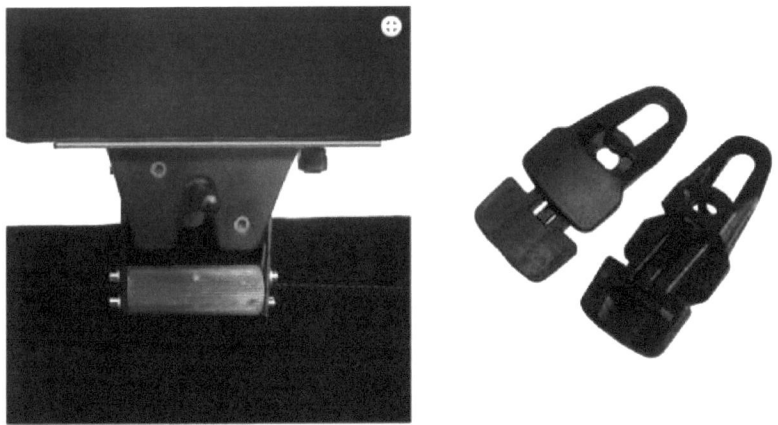

Photo Credit: Gerriets (left)/ MagicFX (right)

DROP POINTS

The drop points refer to the devices or connections that attached the curtain to the flying bar and release the curtain when needed.

For manual systems, the drop points can be a rolling pole with pegs,

BASIC COMPONENTS OF THE KABUKI DROP

Velcro attachments, pins and loops or pins and sleeve.

See "Manual Kabuki Drop Systems" for more details.

Photo Credit: Drape Kings

For electronic systems, the drop points can be linear solenoids, electromagnet locks, gate catch release systems, catches, hooks, clips and pins.

See "Electronic Kabuki Drop Systems" for more details.

TRIGGER MECHANISM

All manual systems are activated by some kind of wire cable or rope that releases the cloth from the drop points. In this case, a human or trained monkey manually pulls the trigger.

See "Manual Kabuki Drop Systems" for more details.

Photo Credit: Gerriets

All electronic systems use some kind of switch to allow an electric current to activate the drop point mechanism.

The electronic Kabuki Drop can also be hooked up to a DMX control panel or other split connectors. DMX or DMX512 (Digital Multiplex) is a standard for digital communication networks that are commonly used to control stage lighting and effects.

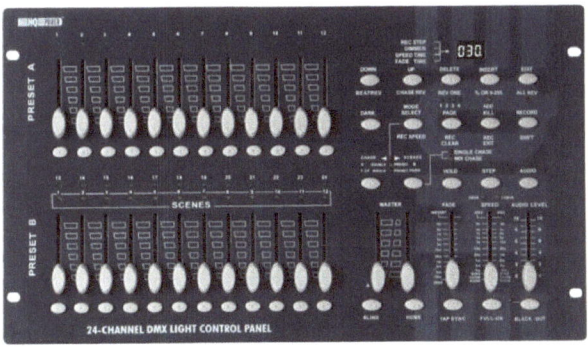

See "Electronic Kabuki Drop Systems" for more details.

MANUAL KABUKI DROP SYSTEMS

There are several ways to build a manual Kabuki Drop, each with a different set-up and system. However, all manual systems are activated by some kind of wire cable or rope that releases the cloth from the drop points. In this case, a human manually pulls the trigger.

The benefits of manual Kabuki Drops are that they are generally reliable with fewer points of failure if set up is done correctly.

They are also inexpensive compared to electronic systems. Depending on the system, the materials used to build the Kabuki Drop and the width of the curtain drop, it can cost as little as $50 to put together (excluding the cost of the curtain). A professionally-made manual system will generally cost below $500 (depending on the width of the curtain drop).

While some people like the tactile activation of the curtain drop, some prefer a more technology-based system that electronic systems offer.

Manual Kabuki Drops also cannot be triggered remotely. The trigger mechanism (pull cord) must be next to or behind the stage, otherwise the running of pull cables at different angles and for long distances can complicate the system unnecessarily.

This article outlines four methods for manual Kabuki Drops.

It would be best to first be familiar with the Basic Components of the Kabuki Drop to better understand the systems explored below.

"Shake & Drop" Kabuki Drop or "Rolling Pole" Kabuki Drop

At the heart of this method, it is essentially the same concept as the traditional Kabuki Drop system using the rotating bamboo pole.

The curtain is held up by a pole that has pegs attached to it. The pole is suspended on the flying bars by ropes in such a way that it can freely rotate. When the pole rotates forward curtain slips off the pegs and onto the floor to effect the Kabuki Drop.

SIDE VIEW

Curtain is attached to pegs

When bamboo pole is rotated forward, curtain falls off pegs and to the floor

Image Credit: Magic Kabuki Drop

Updated versions make use of modern materials as well as hardware components not available in the past.

Instead of using bamboo poles with prongs attached to it, you can make a "rolling pole" with 1.5" aluminum or stainless steel round tubing. The drop points (pegs or prongs) can be welded onto the round tubing or bolts can be threaded through the round tubing and secured in place with nuts.

Pipe-holding brackets, available at good hardware stores, can be used to hold the round tubing in place but provide a loose fit so that the round tubing can freely rotate within the brackets. The pipe-holding brackets can be secured to the flying bar in a variety of ways depending on the design of the specific bracket you use.

Examples of Pipe Holding Brackets

The trigger mechanism can be built using a latch that holds the pole at a specific angle so that the drop points are facing up. Upon release, gravity causes the pole to rotate forward, allowing the curtain to slip off the drop points and drop to the ground.

Examples of Spring Latches

An example of a trigger mechanism using a spring-loaded latch can be viewed in the video shared by user "cforand" in the Control Booth forum (http://www.controlbooth.com) who also provided a PDF for an updated design (although updated with an electronic trigger).

A spring-loaded gate latch is used as the connection point and is released by a pull cord that runs behind the flying bars to the back of the stage.

An alternative design (with more details and measurements) for this method is detailed later in the book in "Roll & Drop Kabuki Drop". It features a simplified spring-loaded trigger mechanism and the pull rope runs off to the side of the stage instead of behind it

"Poor Man's" Kabuki Drop

Also called a "Tearaway", the "Poor Man's" Kabuki Drop is predominantly used for budget-conscious users. However, this curtain drop might also just be all you need in certain situations. Sometimes, you do not need a complicated system if a simple one will suffice.

The "Poor Man's" Kabuki Drop uses Velcro as the main attachment to the flying bar. To "drop" the curtain, the curtain is manually pulled away from the Velcro when needed.

The general rule of thumb for the "Poor Man's" Kabuki Drop is that it is not used for dramatic reveals, but more as a masking piece. However, with creativity, it is possible to create a visually-pleasing reveal with talent onstage performers and choreography.

The "Poor Man's Kabuki Drop can be made in the following way:

Sew a non-adhesive Velcro strip across the entire top edge of the curtain. It is important to sew the hook side (hard side) of the Velcro onto the curtain instead of the loop side (soft side). The reason is that the loop side of the Velcro wears out over time and needs to be replaced. It is much easier to replace when it is not sewn down onto the curtain.

The curtain will be attached to a header that will be secured to the flying bar.

The header is made from 3" nylon webbing and runs the entire width of the cloth. The bottom 1" has a length of Velcro sewn onto the entire length of the header. 1" Grommets are attached to the top 2" of the header, evenly spaced apart.

With this method, the curtain is attached to the header via the Velcro strips and the header is then secured to the flying bar using cable ties threaded through the grommets.

See Basic Components of the Kabuki Drop for a comprehensive view of the curtain preparation, header and grommets.

"Pins & Loops" Kabuki Drop

This is another relatively simple manual Kabuki Drop system that can be built with items that can bought from a good hardware store.

It is called the "Pins & Loops" Kabuki Drop because the system uses a pin and two loops for each drop point.

In this system, the drop points are mounted on a wooden backboard that is secured to the flying bar with clamps or cable ties. Each drop point is made up of two eye screws.

The curtain is prepared with split rings on the grommets. Each split ring is placed between each pair of screw eyes and a pin is placed through the split ring and screw eyes. This holds up the curtain on the backboard.

A pull cord is attached to all the pins and when pulled, causes all the pins to be pulled free from the screw eyes. This releases the split rings and allows the curtain to drop to the floor.

The pull cord is threaded through additional screw eyes attached to the backboard so that the pins and cord do not fall to the floor when it is pulled.

Design plans for this manual Kabuki Drop are detailed later in the book.

"Pins & Sleeve" Kabuki Drop

This method is similar to the "Pins & Loops" Kabuki Drop except the pins are permanently attached to a central main shaft.

MANUAL KABUKI DROP SYSTEMS

The main shaft is made from metal round tubing or rod and the pins are bent metal rods cut to size and welded in a straight line onto the main shaft.

The main shaft with pins sit in a "sleeve" or housing such as a larger metal or PVC round tubing. There are short narrow slots in the base of the housing, just large enough for the pins to extend out of the housing. The main shaft remains sitting in the housing. The slots are also just long enough for the pins to move back a couple of inches.

The curtain is prepared with split rings on the grommets. Each split ring is placed onto each pin extending under the housing.

When the pull cord is pulled, the main shaft moves back. The pins that extend out of slots in the house will also move back with the main shaft. This causes the split rings on the grommets/ curtain to fall off the pins, allowing the curtain to fall to the floor

Magicians will recognize that this system is similar to Al Koran's pencil gimmick used in his Himber Ring routine.

FRONT VIEW

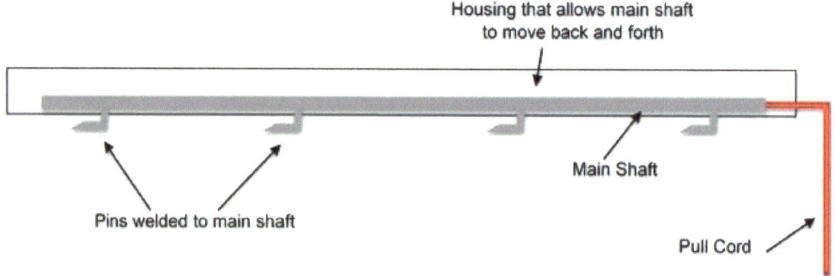

When the pull cord is pulled, the main shaft moves back. The pins that extend out of slots in the house will also move back with the main shaft. This causes the split rings on the grommets/ curtain to fall off the pins, allowing the curtain to fall to the floor

Image Credit: Magic Kabuki Drop

Check out this website for instructions to build a DIY "Pins & Sleeve" Kabuki Drop by John Fromarran at: http://www.johnfromarran.org.uk/kabuki_top_level.html

ELECTRONIC KABUKI DROP SYSTEMS

Modern designs of the Kabuki Drop use electronic systems that use an electric current to activate the drop point mechanism.

The Kabuki Drop can be triggered by a switch and can also be hooked up to a DMX control panel or other split connectors. DMX or DMX512 (Digital Multiplex) is a standard for digital communication networks that are commonly used to control stage lighting and effects.

Photo Credit: Gerriets

The benefits of electronic Kabuki Drop systems are that they can be triggered remotely, far away from stage and each individual drop point can also be controlled individually if desired.

Electronic systems provide precise releases that can be programmed into a DMX control panel and integrated with an elaborate perfectly-timed lighting and special effects sequence.

Some reliability problems with electronic systems that result in a failure for a complete Kabuki Drop include a drop in voltage when firing multiple drop units, faulty electronic parts, communication errors or malfunctions with the DMX program.

Many models of Electronic Kabuki Drops are also noisy with a distinct loud clicking or buzzing sound upon activation.

Electronic Kabuki Drops can be expensive. Renting a system can cost up to hundreds of dollars and purchasing a system will cost thousands.

While each system features different type of catches, latches, pins, hooks and release mechanisms, most electronic kabuki drops generally use a solenoid as the main activation mechanism.

However, the solenoid can take on two forms, namely:

- A Linear Electromechanical Actuator (also known as a Linear Solenoid)
- An Electromagnetic Lock

LINEAR SOLENOID KABUKI DROP SYSTEMS

What is a Solenoid?

In its basic form, a solenoid is a long, thin tight coil of wire that produces a uniform magnetic field inside the coil pocket when an electric current is passed through it.

A Linear Electromechanical Actuator (LEMA), or simply Linear Solenoid, includes a plunger designed to fit into the solenoid coil pocket. This plunger is typically made from a ferrous square or round metal bar.

When an electrical current is passed through the coil of wire, it behaves like an electromagnet and the plunger is "pulled back" or attracted towards the center of the coil by the magnetic flux setup within the coil's body.

It is generally spring-loaded so the plunger returns to its neutral position when the power to the solenoid is cut.

The concept of a linear solenoid is to convert electrical energy into a mechanical pushing or pulling force or motion, hence the term "electromechanical actuator".

Generally, in engineering and in the context of Kabuki Drop systems, when the term solenoid is used, it refers to a linear solenoid.

The solenoid, which is cylindrical in shape, can be purchased at large general hardware stores or electronic parts stores.

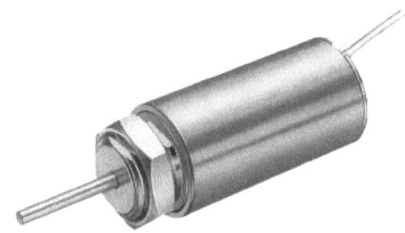

Typical Linear Solenoid

For more detailed technical information on linear solenoids, visit: G.W. LISK Company Inc.

Electronic "Pull Pin" Kabuki Drop

This a basic linear solenoid Kabuki Drop system that has a pin secured to the plunger in the form of a threaded rod that is screwed into the plunger head.

The solenoid cylinder is mounted and encased into a housing (a box made of plastic or metal) and the plunger pin extends out of the housing through a hole drilled through the side of the housing.

The entire housing is clamped onto a truss bar and this serves as the drop point for the Kabuki curtain.

The curtain is hung on the pins of the drop points via grommets fitted across the top edge of the curtain.

A cross section view of the solenoid cylinder is shown below.

Image Credit: Magic Kabuki Drop

When electricity is passed through these solenoids, the plungers retract into the housing, causing the pins to be pulled out of the Kabuki curtain which subsequently falls to the floor.

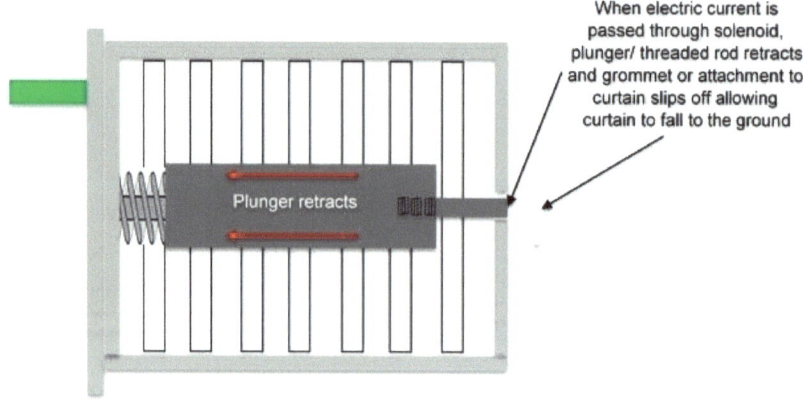

Image Credit: Magic Kabuki Drop

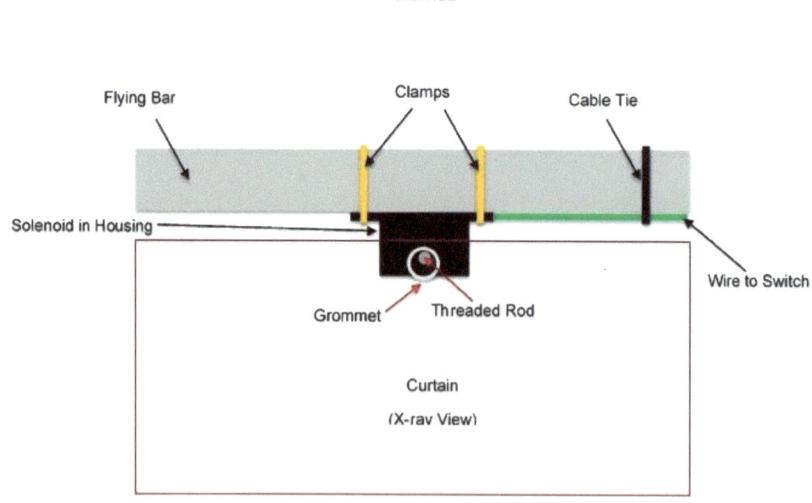

Image Credit: Magic Kabuki Drop

Electronic "Lever Release" Kabuki Drop

A linear solenoid can also be used to release a lever that holds up the Kabuki curtain instead of simply retracting a plunger pin as described in the basic solenoid system above.

It can also be used to pull open a gate latch or custom-fabricated arm.

Here are some examples:

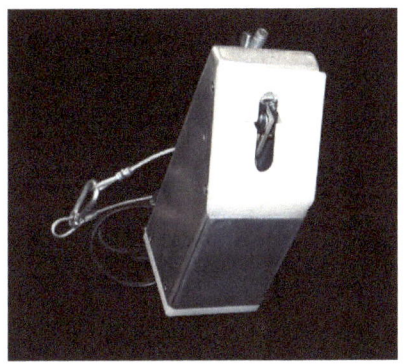

Photo Credit: Sew What? Inc

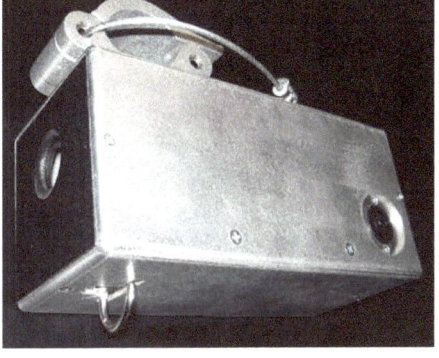

Photo Credit: Chabuki

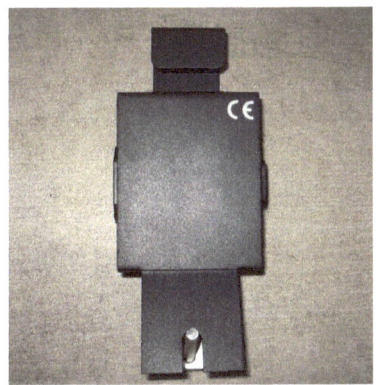

Lever Arm Solenoid Kabuki Drop Manufactured in China

Magic FX's Power Drop
Photo Credit: MagicFX

ELECTRONIC KABUKI DROP SYSTEMS

Release Solenoid Previously Manufactured by Flints

Photo Credit: Rent What? Inc

Also check out:

- A Patent for an <u>Electronic Lever Release Kabuki Drop</u> by Jesus Chuy Fragoso.
  (http://www.google.com/patents/US20070234833)

- Linear Solenoid Used to Release Safety Pin of a Marine Shackle by Tom Howard (<u>As posted in the Blue Room forum http://www.blue-room.org.uk/index.php?showtopic=31397</u>)

- Linear Solenoid used to Open a Gate Lock that Releases a Curtain by <u>Connection Pointe Production Team</u>.
  (http://cpccproduction.org/wpsite/2011/08/24/creating-take-heart-live/)

Electronic "Shake & Drop" or "Rolling Pole" Kabuki Drop

This is a modern version of the traditional "rolling pole" Kabuki Drop but uses a linear solenoid to trigger a spring loaded gate latch to rotate the pole with drop points instead of a pull cord.

Check out a Double Kabuki Drop in action using an electronically-powered modern day "Rolling Pole" Kabuki Drop system in the video at: https://www.youtube.com/watch?v=B-pK4wBptWQ

One manufacturer that offers a variation of this system is Showtex. Their system is described in their operation manual at: http://www.showtex.com/uploads/tx_miashowtex/8150_Kabuki_Manual_EN.pdf

The Showtex system uses a solenoid system that drops an aluminum bar with drop points (pegs) at a downward angle to effect the curtain drop.

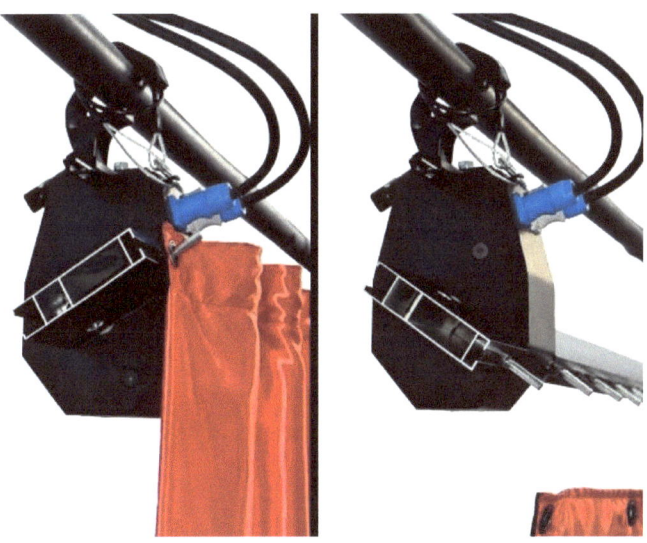

Show Tex Kabuki Drop
Photo Credit: Showtex

Electronic "Pins & Loops" Kabuki Drop System

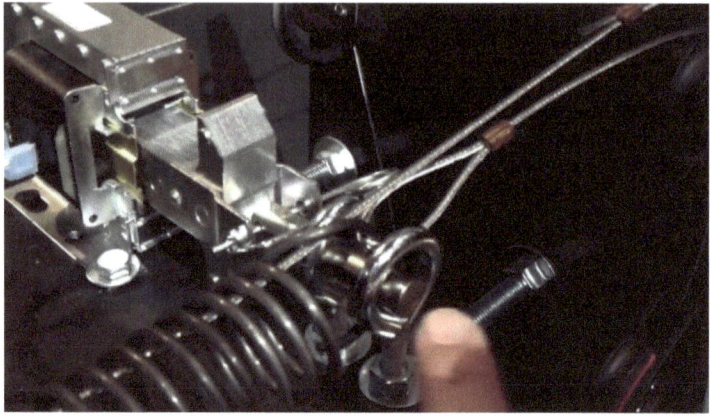

This video describes an electronic version of the "Pins & Loops" Kabuki Drop system. Instead of a pull cord as used in the manual version, this system uses a tensioned-spring to pull all the pins from the loops to release the curtain.

Unlike all other electronic systems, which requires the use of multiple individual solenoid drop point units, this system uses only one linear solenoid that keeps the spring pulled open when the Kabuki Drop is set up. When triggered, the solenoid releases the spring that pulls all the pins from the loops and activates the curtain drop.

ELECTROMAGNETIC LOCK KABUKI DROP SYSTEMS

Electromagnetic Kabuki Drop systems do not use linear solenoids but use solenoids as an electromagnet lock.

Unlike permanent magnets that are magnetic in their natural state, electromagnets are ferrous metals that only become magnetized when an electrical current is passed through them.

This characteristic allows electromagnets to act as a locking system when they are energized. When the electrical current is cut, the electromagnets magnetic powers cease allowing for a release in the locking system.

This is similar to the system used in electromagnetic doors in buildings for security purposes.

The benefits of an electromagnetic lock Kabuki Drop system are that it an easier electronic system to build as compared to linear solenoid systems. It is also easier to set up than most other systems and it is relatively silent when activated.

The downside is that it uses a lot of electricity and the constant electric current required to keep the electromagnets on can shorten the lives of the power cables.

"Electromagnetic Lock" Kabuki Drop

As the name suggests, a basic electromagnetic lock Kabuki Drop system uses electromagnets as a lock mechanism.

Each drop point comprises of a holding magnet (or electromagnet) and an armature plate.

Holding Magnet

Armature Plate

The armature plate is a ferromagnetic plate with a fixing hole that allows it to be attached to the kabuki curtain. It is usually attached to the cloth via rubber grommets.

The holding magnet will possess magnetic properties when energized. When the current passes through the magnet, it will cause the armature plate to be attracted to the magnet. This creates a locking action that holds the kabuki curtain in place.

During set-up, the holding magnet is clamped onto the flying bar. The armature plate, that is securely fastened onto the curtain is then attached, one by one, onto the respective holding magnets by means of magnetic attraction.

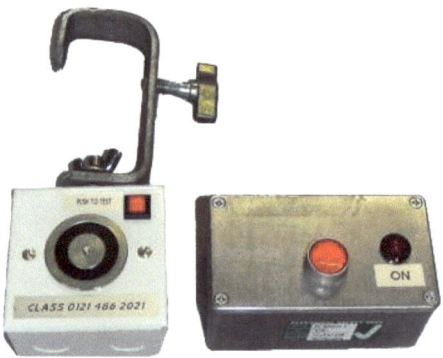

Photo Credit: Event Staging and Presentation Support Ltd

When all the drop points are set up, the flying bar is raised up above the stage and the curtain is suspended open.

Upon the cutting off of the electric current supply, the holding magnet demagnetizes and releases its grip on the curtain, thus allowing the curtain to fall to the floor.

"Electromagnetic Catch Release" Kabuki Drop

This system uses an electromagnetic lock system in a different way.

Instead of directly using the holding magnet to attach the curtain to the drop point, the holding magnet holds up a hook with arm lever where the curtain hangs from.

The magnet releases the hook with arm lever when electricity is applied to the unit; a sprung plate ensures release even if a light load is applied.

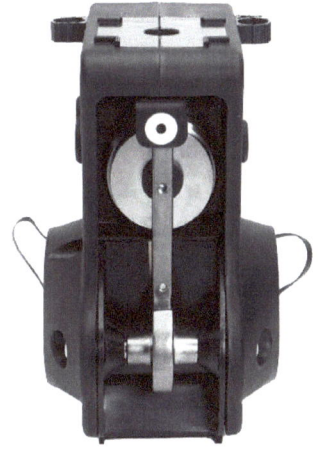

Electro Kabuki: EK2

Photo Credit: Electro Kabuki

Powadrop

Photo Credit: Powa Productions

DOUBLE KABUKI DROP SYSTEM

As the name implies, the Double Kabuki Drop features two drop activation sequences. The curtain first starts off gathered or rolled up and is held in place at the top of the stage proscenium (on the flying bars).

Activating the curtain drop the first time will open up the curtain so that it covers the stage. Activating the curtain drop a second time will drop the curtain to the floor revealing what is on stage.

A Double Kabuki Drop can be activated either manually or electronically. Any system of drop points can be adapted as a double drop.

The underlying method for any double curtain drop is the need for two sets of drop points. There also needs to be an extra cloth "hammock" that will hold the curtain gathered up in place at the start.

The cloth "hammock" acts as a basket for the curtain. One long edge of the cloth "hammock" is permanently secured to the flying bar or Kabuki system support bar/ backboard (if there is one). The other long edge of the cloth "hammock" is attached to the additional drop points of the Double Kabuki Drop units.

ULTIMATE KABUKI DROP RESOURCE

SIDE VIEW

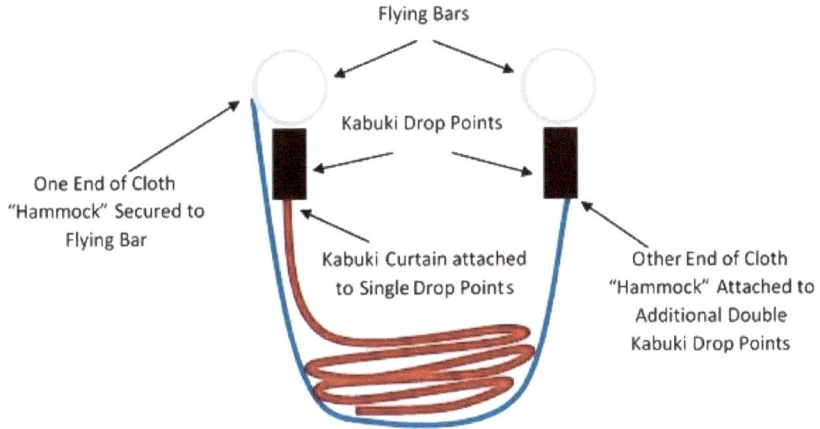

Image Credit: Magic Kabuki Drop

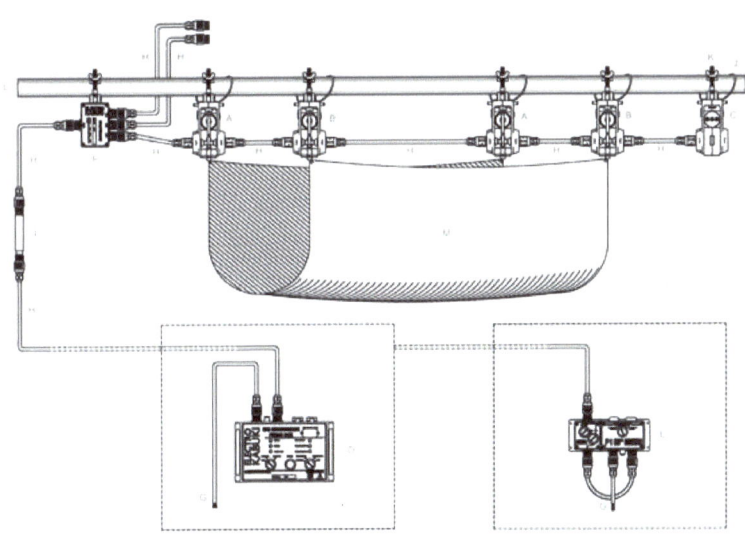

Alternative Set-up for the Double Kabuki Drop on the Same Flying Bar
Image Credit: Electro Kabuki

DOUBLE KABUKI DROP SYSTEM

The first drop releases the cloth "hammock" so that it falls open and allows the curtain to drop open.

The second drop releases the curtain to fall to the floor.

Instead of a cloth "hammock", you can also use multiple straps or even wire cables to hold up the gathered/ rolled up curtain. If the curtain is very long (height), you may need to mount the Double Kabuki Drop points on another flying bar so that the cloth "hammock" forms a large "basket"

Reference:

- "Plans for a Double Kabuki Drop" by Kate Wicker, <u>Technical Design Solutions for Theatre, Volume 3</u>

BUILD, BUY OR RENT KABUKI DROP SYSTEMS

If you require a Kabuki Drop for your next show, production or special event, you essentially have three options:

1. Build a System
2. Buy a System
3. Rent a System

The option you choose depends on your needs, constraints and preference.

If you are producing a multi-million dollar touring concert, you should go with a high-end professional system that is supported with an experienced team.

However, there are many smaller events and shows that do not require or have the budget for professional systems with a team. In which case, a DIY solution or renting a system for a one-off event may be a better option.

CONSIDERATIONS

The choice of building, buying or renting the Kabuki Drop depends on a variety of determining factors. Some questions to ask yourself include:

- How large is the Kabuki Drop?
- What sort of fabric is used for the curtain?
- How many times will the Kabuki Drop be used?
- Is there ample time to set up and test the Kabuki Drop at the venue?
- Is the Kabuki Drop going to be used at a fixed location or as part of a touring show that needs to be set-up/ tore down frequently?
- Do you have the manpower required to set up/ tear down and activate the Kabuki Drop?
- How significant is the role that the Kabuki Drop plays in your show, production or event?
- How much time do you have before you need the Kabuki Drop for your show, production or event?
- Do you have the skills and tools necessary to build a Kabuki Drop?
- Do you have the skills to troubleshoot, maintain and use a professional Kabuki Drop system?
- What is your budget?

Answers to the above questions will help determine which option may be more suitable for you.

<u>Budget</u>

One of the biggest factors to consider will be the budget that you have to work with.

There are two factors for financial consideration. One is the initial investment and the other is the ongoing cost.

- Building your own Kabuki Drop system will generally cost the least.

- Renting a Kabuki Drop system will be more expensive than building one but you would incur rental cost each time you require it. This cost can accumulate if you are using the system multiple times.

- Buying a Kabuki Drop system requires the highest initial investment with some ongoing costs such as maintenance or storage. However, if you are using the system multiple times, the investment may be worth it as the costs are amortized over a period of time/ uses.

Here are specific considerations for each option:

BUILDING A KABUKI DROP

While building a Kabuki Drop does not require the technical skills of the "American Chopper" team, an aptitude for wood work, handling of tools and building of things as well as the availability of a properly equipped workshop are a must.

The size of the Kabuki drop can be a factor when building a system. If the curtain is very large, you will need sufficient space to build and test the drop.

Your time should also be factored into this consideration. You will need time to design, plan, build and test the system. If you do not have a lead time sufficient to build and test the system, you are likely better off buying or renting a system.

Research

The first step is to research for Kabuki Drop methods, systems and designs.

Some resources include:

BUILD, BUY OR RENT KABUKI DROP SYSTEMS

- Online 'how-to' site that lists simple steps on making a basic Kabuki Drop

  http://www.ehow.com/how_12181328_make-kabuki-curtain-drop.html

- User contributed 'how-to' site that lists steps on making a Kabuki Drop

  http://paperclip.rcs.ac.uk/index.php/Macbeth_2013

- Online/ Physical Technical Theatre Book that details Kabuki Drop System

  https://www.safaribooksonline.com/library/view/technical-design-solutions/9780415824293/08_Chapter7.html#c6

- User-created Website with details on User's DIY Kabuki Drop

  http://www.johnfromarran.org.uk/kabuki_top_level.html

- Forum Thread with discussion on Making Kabuki Drop (with links to videos and pictures)

  http://www.controlbooth.com/threads/drop-curtain-system.23911/

Choosing, Designing & Building the System

Your research should help you decide on the Kabuki Drop method you can/ want to build; for example, whether it is a manual or electromechanical linear solenoid system.

Plan out exactly what you need and how to build the system. This includes having a set of building plans, materials & tools list.

Come up with a production timeline to ensure you have a timetable for building, testing and troubleshooting the system.

If you do not have a theatre venue to work in, it is advisable set-up some kind of suspended horizontal support to replicate a flying bar to test the curtain drop under "real working" conditions.

Get familiar with the system. Understand its idiosyncrasies and learn how to make adjustments and troubleshoot as necessary to get the system working perfectly.

BUYING A KABUKI DROP

The benefits of buying a Kabuki Drop from a manufacturer is that you are investing in a professional system.

A professional system means it has been developed with expertise, research & development, prototyping, time and resources. You are generally guaranteed a better system than one you could build in a few days. But, understandably, it comes with a higher price.

You will likely only buy a system if you are going to use the Kabuki Drop on a regular basis or have a venue that you would like to install the Kabuki Drop in as a permanent special effect fixture.

Research

As always, the first step is to research what options are available to you.

Professional systems can include manual and electronic Kabuki Drops. Get some basic understanding of the different types of systems on the market and compare their pros & cons. For example:

- Some systems may be elaborate and can be controlled digitally through a DMX control board but require a long set-up time and are expensive.

- Some systems are very basic but inexpensive.

- Some systems may be lightweight and pack small while some systems require ATA cases to transport the equipment safely.

- Some systems are very easy to set-up while some may require a bit more expertise and experience.

Be sure to select a system that suits your needs and not one that seems the most expensive or has the most features.

Contact the Manufacturer/ Reseller of Kabuki Drop System

Contact the manufacturers or resellers of different systems and request for product info and prices, if the information is not available online.

A list of manufacturers of professional Kabuki Drop systems include:

Manual Systems:

- Pro Magic Kabuki Drop System

Liner Solenoid Systems:

- Gerriets
- Rose Brand
- Chabuki
- iWeiss
- Magic FX
- Rent What? Inc.
- Showtex
- Effects Technologies

- SGA
- Joseph C. Hansen Co.

Electromagnetic Lock Systems:

- Electro Kabuki
- ESP Support

Buy the System and Learn How to Use it

Once you have all the pertinent information on hand and have worked out your budget, purchase the system.

Note, it is will still take some time for the delivery of the Kabuki Drop and you will need additional time to make the curtains and learn how to use the system. Be sure to factor this into your lead time when buying the Kabuki Drop.

RENTING A KABUKI DROP

If you require a Kabuki Drop for a one-off event or show, renting the system may be the best option.

If you are organizing an event and have an appointed event producer, you can have him/her source for a vendor for you and make all the necessary arrangements.

If you are self-producing an event or show and require just the Kabuki Drop, you can source for an event production or technical service provider. You can also look for a company that specializes in drapes for theatrical productions.

Do a Google search or ask for recommendations if you have any friends in the event or theatre industry.

BUILD, BUY OR RENT KABUKI DROP SYSTEMS

<u>What to Look Out For?</u>

Renting the system generally includes the support team to set up/ tear down and execute the curtain drop so it is a hassle-free option.

As you will unlikely be using the Kabuki Drop system yourself, you do not really need to be concerned with the type of the Kabuki Drop System used.

What is more important is the reliability of the provider as well as the system they are using.

Some questions to ask a potential rental provider include:

- What is the cost of the Kabuki Drop (based on the size of curtain you need)?

- How long will it take to set up?

- How experienced are they in Kabuki Drops? What past shows/ events have they done?

- What type of Kabuki Drop system are they using? Any particular brand?

- How reliable is the system and what happens if the system fails or the curtain does not drop completely?

Based on the answers given, you should be able to assess which company would be best for you.

Here is a quick guide as to help you decide whether you should build, buy or rent a Kabuki Drop System:

Determining Factors	BUILD	BUY	RENT
Large Kabuki Drop	No	Yes	Yes
Heavy Kabuki Drop Fabric	No	Yes	Yes
Repeated Use of System	Yes	Yes	No
Use of System at Fixed Location	Yes	Yes	No
Manpower for Set-up/ Tear Down/ Activation	Yes	Yes	No
Significant Role of Kabuki Drop in Show/ Event	No	Yes	Yes
Long Lead Time to Production/ Event	Yes	Yes	No
Possess Skills & Tools for Building Kabuki Drop	Yes	No	No
Possess Skills for Troubleshooting/ Maintenance	Yes	Yes	No
High Budget	No	Yes	Yes

BIBLIOGRAPHY

HISTORY OF THE KABUKI THEATRE/ KABUKI STAGECRAFT & CURTAIN DROP/ EVOLUTION OF THE CURTAIN DROP

- "Edo period." Wikipedia. Retrieved on 15 Feb 2015.
- "Expression in Kabuki: Kabuki Maku (curtains)." Invitation to Kabuki. Japan Arts Council. Retrieved on 15 Feb 2015.
- Hamatani, Hiroshi. "The Nature of Kabuki and Bunraku Scenery." The Asiatic Society of Japan. Retrieved on 15 Feb 2015.
- Shun'ichirō, Kanai. "History of Kabuki Sets." GloPAD. Japanese Performing Arts Resource Center. Retrieved on 15 Feb 2015.
- "Kabuki." Wikipedia. Retrieved on 15 Feb 2015.
- Lombard, Frank Alanson. "Kabuki: A History." TheatreHistory.com. Retrieved on 15 Feb 2015.
- Leiter, Samuel L. "Historical Dictionary of Japanese Traditional Theatre." Scarecrow Press, 2006. Retrieved on 15 Feb 2015.
- Petersen, David. "An Invitation to Kagura: Hidden Gem of the Traditional Japanese Performing Arts." 2007. Retrieved on 15 Feb 2015.
- Leiter, Samuel L. "A Kabuki Reader: History and Performance." M.E. Sharpe, 2002. Retrieved on 15 Feb 2015.
- Leiter, Samuel L, and Brandon, James R. "Kabuki Plays on Stage: Darkness and Desire, 1804-1864." University of Hawaii Press, 2002. Retrieved on 9 Feb 2015.

- Halford, Aubrey S, and Halford, Giovanna M. "The Kabuki Handbook: A Guide to Understanding and Appreciation." C. E. Tuttle Company, 1956. Retrieved on 9 Feb 2015.
- Ernst, Earle. "The Kabuki Theatre." University of Hawaii Press, 1974. Retrieved on 18 Mar 2015.
- Leiter, Samuel L. "The Art of Kabuki: Five Famous Plays." Courier Corporation, 1999. Retrieved on 18 Mar 2015.
- Scott, Adolphe Clarence. "The Kabuki Theatre of Japan." Courier Corporation, 1955. Retrieved on 18 Mar 2015.
- Reynolds, Andy. "The Tour Book, Second Edition: How to Get Your Music on the Road." Cengage Learning, 2013. Retrieved on 9 Feb 2015.
- Wood, Bethany, and Hamilton, Tim. "Elements of Production." Narukami – The Thunder God (University of Wisconsin – Madison, University Theatre's Spring 2010 Production). Retrieved on 18 Mar 2015.
- "Kabuki Glossary (H~J)." Kabuki21.com. Retrieved on 15 Feb 2015.
- "The appearance and utilities of a traditional set for the Kabuki performance of Aoto Zōshi Hana no Niskiki-e by Kawatake Mokuami." PDF. Retrieved on 18 Mar 2015.

BASIC COMPONENTS OF THE KABUKI DROP

- "Screen Frames." Screenchange.com. Chris Hitchens Ltd Screen and Stage Engineering. Retrieved on 20 Mar 2015.
- Megan. "The Art of the Kabuki." Sew What? Inc. Blog. Retrieved on 15 Mar 2015.
- "Grommet." Wikipedia. Retrieved on 20 Mar 2015.
- "How to Easily Install a Grommet in Fabric by www.creativedish.com." YouTube video. Retrieved on 18 Mar 2015.

BIBLIOGRAPHY

- Liz, Johnson. "How to Install Metal Grommets." Sew4Home. Retrieved on 20 Mar 2015.
- "Kabuki Drop System Operation Manual." Risam for show. Gerriets. Retrieved on 20 Feb 2015.
- Lynda. "Focus On: Single Kabuki Drapes." Sew What? Inc. Blog. Retrieved on 15 Mar 2015.
- "Gerriets." Gerriets. Retrieved on 20 Mar 2015.

MANUAL KABUKI DROP SYSTEMS

- "Kabuki Curtain Drop (How To Build a Manual Drop." YouTube video. Retrieved on 18 Mar 2015.
- "Drop curtain system." ControlBooth forum. Retrieved on 18 Mar 2015.
- "The Ins And Outs Of The Kabuki." Sew What? Inc. Retrieved on 15 Mar 2015.
- Lynda. "Focus On: Poor Man's Kabuki." Sew What? Inc. Blog. Retrieved on 15 Mar 2015.
- "Kabuki Drops." PAPERCLIP. Retrieved on 15 Feb 2015.
- "Cloth Drop." Blue Room technical forum. Retrieved on 18 Mar 2015.
- "CLS Studding Timber Suppliers." Chiltern Timber Supplies Ltd. Retrieved on 19 Mar 2015.
- "DIY Kabuki Drop." Johnfromarran.org.uk. Retrieved on 15 Mar 2015.

ELECTRONIC KABUKI DROP SYSTEMS

- "Linear Solenoid Actuator." Basic Electronics Tutorials. Retrieved on 18 Mar 2015.

- "What Is A Solenoid Plunger?" wiseGEEK. Conjecture Corporation. Retrieved on 18 Mar 2015.

- "Design Guide for Linear Solenoids." G.W. Lisk Company Inc. Retrieved on 15 Mar 2015.

- "Solenoid." Wikipedia. Retrieved on 17 Mar 2015.

- "Electro Holding Magnet." Industrial Magnetic Systems. Kendrion. Retrieved on 20 Mar 2015.

- "Electromagnetic lock." Wikipedia. Retrieved on 17 Mar 2015.

- "Kabuki Solenoid." Innovation Productions. Retrieved on 21 Mar 2015.

- "Holding Magnet." Flints Theatrical Chandlers. Flint Hire & Supply LTD. Retrieved on 21 Mar 2015.

- "Armature Plates." Flints Theatrical Chandlers. Flint Hire & Supply LTD. Retrieved on 21 Mar 2015.

- Fragoso, Jesus Chuy. "Kabuki Stage Setting Release Device." Google Patent. Retrieved on 20 Mar 2015.

- "Double Kabuki Drop Explanation." YouTube video. Retrieved on 17 Feb 2015.

- "Electro Kabuki EK2 Series." Electro Kabuki. Magnet Schultz Ltd in England. Retrieved on 19 Feb 2015.

- "Kabuki G2 Curtain Drop System Overview." Gerriets. Retrieved on 21 Mar 2015.

- "Kabuki G2 Curtain Drop System Components." Gerriets. Retrieved on 21 Mar 2015.

- "Kabuki 50." ShowTex. Retrieved on 21 Mar 2015.

DOUBLE KABUKI DROP SYSTEM

- "BYU Men's Basketball 2013 Kabuki Drop." YouTube video. Retrieved on 18 Mar 2015.

- Lynda. "Focus On: Double Kabuki Drapes." Sew What? Inc. Blog. Retrieved on 15 Mar 2015.

MANUFACTURERS

Manual Systems

- Pro Magic Kabuki Drop System

Linear Solenoid Kabuki Drop Systems

- Gerriets
- Rose Brand
- Chabuki
- iWeiss
- Magic FX
- Rent What? Inc.
- Showtex
- Effects Technologies
- SGA
- Joseph C. Hansen Co.

Electromagnetic Lock Kabuki Drop Systems

- Electro Kabuki
- ESP Support

DIY KABUKI DROP SYSTEMS

There are several ways to build a manual Kabuki Drop, each with a different set-up and system. However, all manual systems are activated by some kind of wire cable or rope that releases the cloth from the drop points. In this case, a human manually pulls the trigger.

The benefits of manual Kabuki Drops are that they are generally reliable with fewer points of failure if set up is done correctly. They are also inexpensive compared to electronic systems.

Depending on the system, the materials used to build the Kabuki Drop and the width of the curtain drop, it can cost as little as $50 to put together (excluding the cost of the curtain). A professionally-made manual system will generally cost below $500 (depending on the width of the curtain drop).

While some people like the tactile activation of the curtain drop, some prefer a more technology-based system that electronic systems offer. Manual Kabuki Drops also cannot be triggered remotely. The trigger mechanism (pull cord) must be next to or behind the stage, otherwise the running of pull cables at different angles and for long distances can complicate the system unnecessarily.

Six manual Kabuki Drop systems & designs are detailed in this book, including:

- "World's Easiest" Drop
- "The Peel" Drop
- "The Pull" Drop
- "Pin & Loop" Drop
- "Pull Back" Drop
- "Roll & Drop" Drop

Before building any Kabuki Drop system, it is important to be familiar with the basic components of a manual system. Refer back to the chapter on "Basic Components of the Kabuki Drop".

WORLD'S EASIEST CURTAIN DROP

This reveal falls under the "absurdly simple" category. However, its simplicity means that it is 100% fail-safe and easy to make.

Essentially, a length of aluminum round tubing or PVC pipe or is inserted through the top hem of the curtain so that about 12" of the pole extends out from either side of the width of the cloth.

The curtain is extended vertically and stretched out. Each end of the pole is held in place on some kind of vertical support. Vertical supports can be in the form of:

- Vertical Truss Columns
- Lighting Stand Tripod
- Scaffolding Towers
- Ladders

When it comes time to drop the curtain, one person on each side of the pole dislodges the pole from the vertical support and allows the pole with curtain to drop to the floor.

WHAT YOU NEED

1" Aluminum Round Tubing (2mm thick) or 1.5" PVC Pipe (2mm thick)

The diameter and thickness of the pole depends on the size and weight of the curtain you are using.

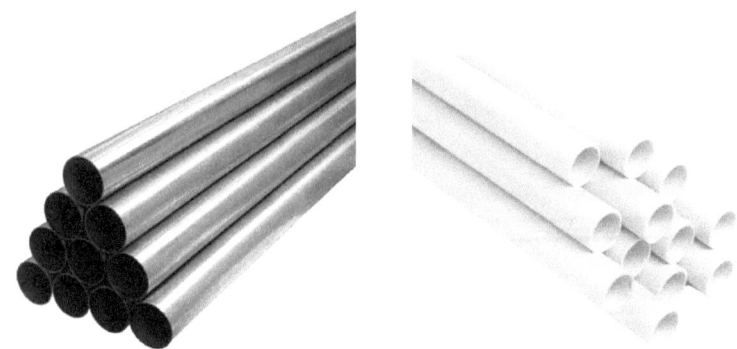

Cut the tubing or pipe to the length you require based on the following measurements. Determine the width of the curtain you will be dropping. Add 2' to this measurement and that would be the width of your pole.

So, if the curtain you are dropping is 24ft wide, the pole would be 26' in length.

If the poles are not long enough or you need to transport the poles easily, you can try to look for connectors to connect two shorter poles together to make a long pole.

You can also buy a short section of a pole just slightly larger in diameter and fit it over the two ends of the connecting poles. This will act as a sleeve to hold the connecting ends of the poles together.

Use a bolt and nut through each end of the connector and through the connecting poles to hold them securely together. Insert the bolts in opposite directions for a more secure lock. See Fig 1.

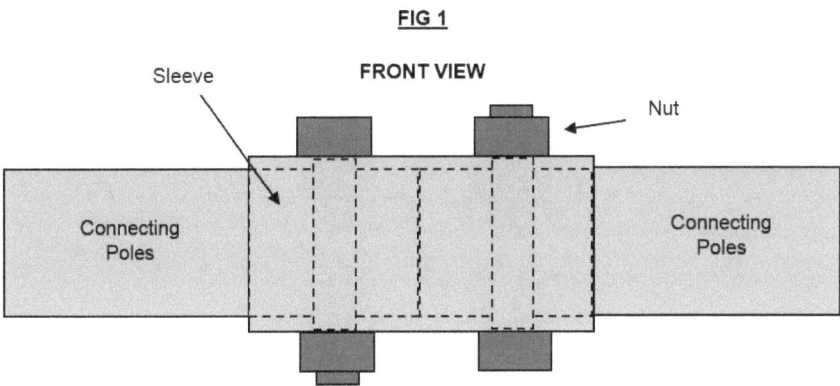

FIG 1

Medium to Large-sized G-Clamps

There are standard clamps that you can buy from hardware stores.

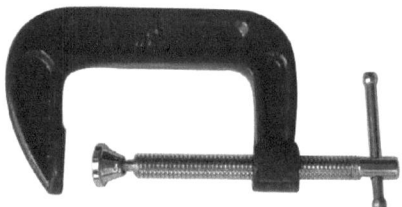

Curtain

The way to prepare the curtain is to fold over the top edge to form a "tube pocket" before sewing it down. The "tube pocket" should be large enough to accommodate the diameter of the pole.

After the aluminum tubing or PVC pipe are inserted into the tube pocket, hand stitch the ends shut. You can also sew strips of Velcro to close the pocket shut so that the pole can be easily removed.

SET-UP & PERFORMANCE

The ends of the pole can be held in place on the vertical supports with G-clamps that are clamped onto the vertical support. The ends of the pole simply rest on the G-clamps.

To activate the curtain drop, two people on ladders literally lift off the ends of the pole off the G-Clamps and drops the curtain to the floor.

If you want a more remote dislodge of the pole, you can drill a hole at either end of the pole. Thread a length of rope through the hole and tie if off allowing the rest of the rope to drop the floor. In this method, the two people pull the rope to dislodge the ends of the pole to activate the curtain drop. See Fig 2.

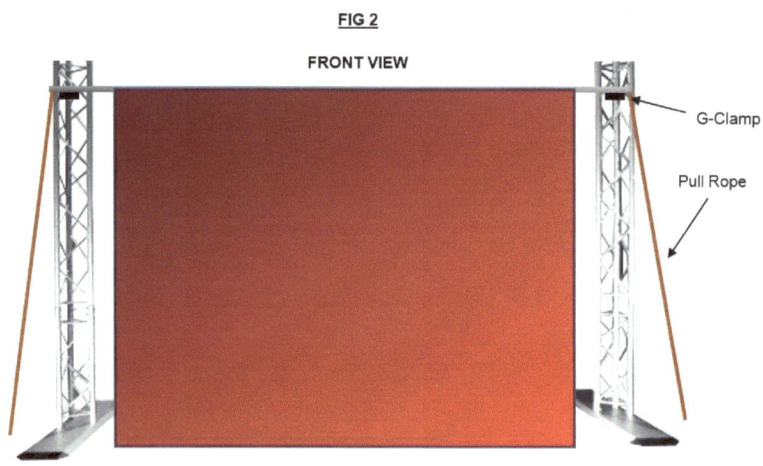

The ends of the poles can be secured to the G-clamps by tying them down with rope before the show. This is just as a security measure so that the pole/ curtain does not accidentally dislodge prematurely.

"THE PEEL" DROP

This reveal is also known as "Poor Man's" Kabuki Drop or "Tearaway" and it is simple to put together and execute. I offer several original design considerations here to make it easier for you to fabricate this curtain drop.

Essentially, the curtain is attached to a header with Velcro that is secured to the flying bar. To activate the curtain drop, a person takes hold of a pull rope and runs across the stage, in front of or behind the curtain, tearing (pulling) down the curtain in the process.

The "Peel" Drop is predominantly used for budget-conscious users. However, this curtain drop might also just be all you need in certain situations. Sometimes, you do not need a complicated system if a simple one will suffice.

The general rule of thumb for the "Poor Man's" Kabuki Drop is that it is not used for dramatic reveals, but more as a masking piece.

However, with creativity, it is possible to create a visually-pleasing reveal with talent onstage performers and choreography.

WHAT YOU NEED

1" Non-Adhesive Velcro

3" Nylon Webbing Header

See the chapter on "Basic Components of the Manual Kabuki Drop"

Heavy Duty Cable Ties

8mm wide cable ties will be used to secure the header to the flying bar.

Curtain

Sew the non-adhesive Velcro strip onto the entire top edge of the curtain. It is important to sew the hook side (hard side) of the Velcro onto the curtain instead of the loop side (soft side).

The reason is that the loop side of the Velcro wears out over time and needs to be replaced. It is much easier to replace when it is not sewn down onto the curtain which is delicate.

Note: It is not recommended to use Velcro with delicate fabrics or fabrics that get snagged by Velcro easily.

Attach a 1" grommet on either end of the top edge of the curtain, right through the Velcro. This is for you to tie a pull rope on one end of the cloth, depending on which side you want the curtain to be peeled down from.

This pull rope will make the "peel" drop look nice but more importantly will protect the curtain from tearing if it is constantly being pulled down from the bottom of the curtain. See Fig 1.

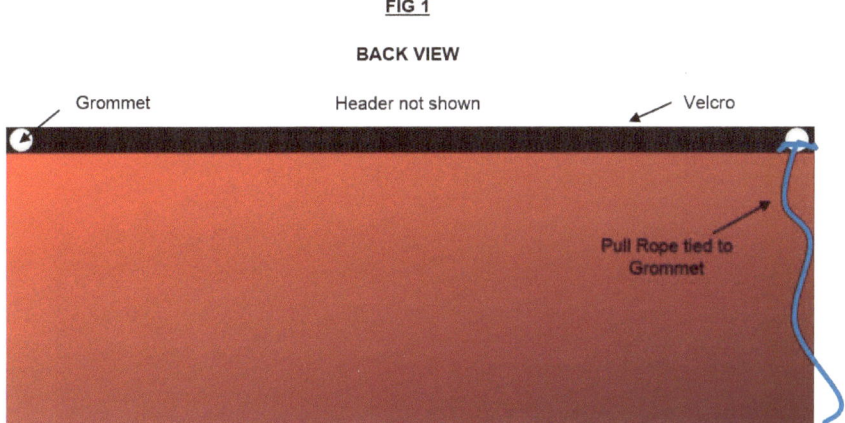

FIG 1

BACK VIEW

SET-UP & PERFORMANCE

Attach the curtain to the header via the Velcro strips. Attach the curtain with header to the flying bar by threading the heavy duty

"THE PEEL" DROP

cable ties through the grommets of the header.

To activate the curtain drop, a person grabs hold of the pull rope and runs across the stage, either in front of or behind the curtain, and "peels" the curtain off the header.

An alternative design is to have two curtains instead of one. Each curtain is attached to its own header and they meet in the middle of the stage.

Each curtain has one pull rope tied to a grommet.

In this case, two people each grab one pull rope and run from the center of the stage to the side wings, peeling the curtain away from the center of the stage for a very visually pleasing reveal. See Fig 2.

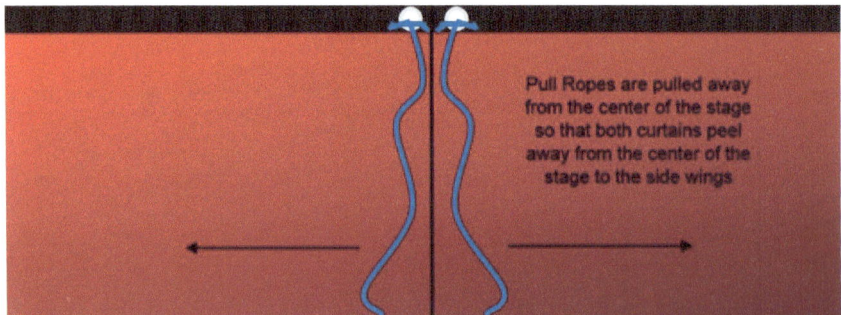

**FIG 2
BACK VIEW**

Header not shown

Pull Ropes are pulled away from the center of the stage so that both curtains peel away from the center of the stage to the side wings

"THE PULL" DROP

This reveal is similar to the "The Peel" Drop except that a person does not have to run across the stage to drop the curtain.

Instead of a strip of Velcro that runs the full length of the curtain, the drop points consist of several tabs of Velcro. This system allows one person at each side of the cloth to pull the curtain while remaining at the side wings of the stage.

Check out "The Peel" Drop in the previous chapter to fully understand this method.

WHAT YOU NEED

1" Non-Adhesive Velcro

3" Nylon Webbing Header

See the chapter on "Basic Components of the Manual Kabuki Drop"

Heavy Duty Cable Ties

8mm wide cable ties will be used to secure the header to the flying bar.

Curtain

Instead of sewing Velcro on the entire top edge of the curtain, you will sew Velcro tabs, each measuring 1" x 1.5" long. These Velcro tabs are evenly spaced out about 4 – 5ft apart from each other, depending on the weight of the curtain you are dropping.

Do not put too many Velcro tabs as too many tabs will make it difficult to pull the curtain down.

It is important to sew the hook side (hard side) of the Velcro onto the curtain instead of the loop side (soft side). The reason is that the loop side of the Velcro wears out over time and needs to be replaced. It is much easier to replace when it is not sewn down onto the curtain which is delicate.

Note: It is not recommended to use Velcro with delicate fabrics or fabrics that get snagged by Velcro easily.

ULTIMATE KABUKI DROP RESOURCE

Attach a 1" grommet on either end of the top edge of the curtain, right through the Velcro. Tie a pull rope on both grommets.

The pull ropes will be used to pull the curtain down but more importantly, protect the curtain from tearing from constant use. See Fig 1.

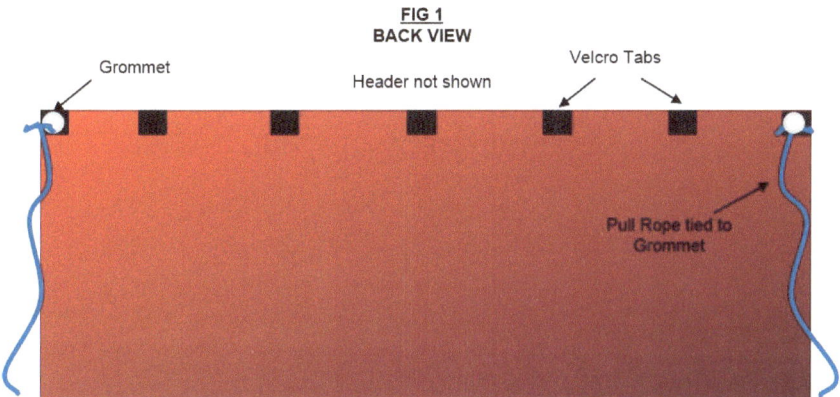

SET-UP & PERFORMANCE

Attach the curtain to the header via the Velcro tabs. Attach the curtain with header to the flying bar by threading the heavy duty cable ties through the grommets of the header.

To activate the curtain drop, two people each grab one pull rope at the side of the stage. Together, they give the rope a sharp tug and the curtain will be pulled down, tab by tab.

The resulting drop will look like a tear-away from the sides to the center of the stage, which is quite unique and visually pleasing.

"PINS & LOOPS" DROP

This is a system that can be activated by just one person with the pull of a cord.

In this system, the drop points are mounted on a wooden backboard that is secured to the flying bar. Each drop point is made up of two eye screws.

The curtain is prepared with split rings on the grommets. Each split ring is placed between each pair of screw eyes and a pin is placed through the split ring and screw eyes. This holds up the curtain to the backboard.

A pull cord is attached to all the pins and when pulled, causes all the pins to be pulled free from the screw eyes.

This releases the split rings and allows the curtain to drop to the floor.

ULTIMATE KABUKI DROP RESOURCE

FRONT VIEW

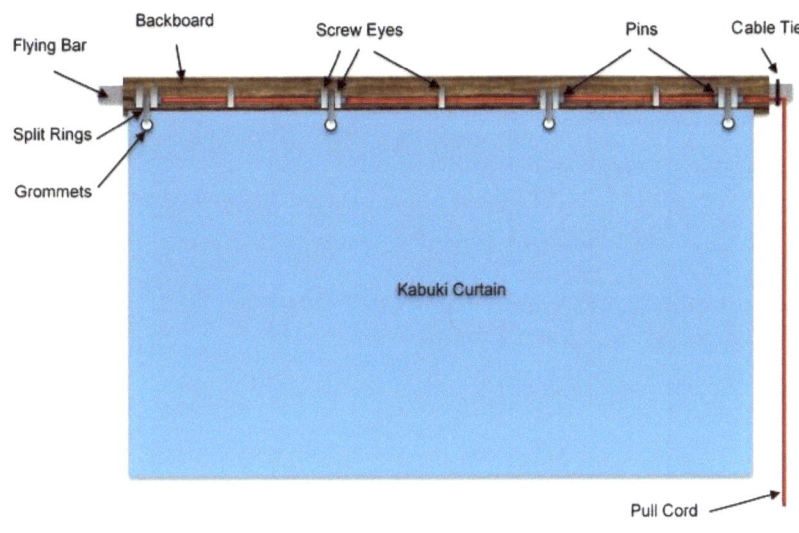

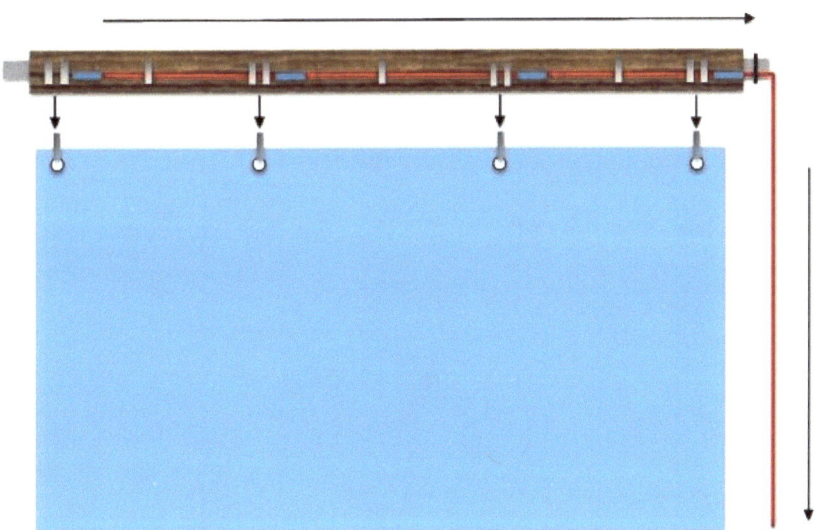

When pull cord is pulled, pins come free of screw eyes, allowing curtain to drop to the floor

WHAT YOU NEED

You will need the following materials to build this system (based on a 24ft wide curtain):

1" x 3" Lumber

This will form the backboard of the Kabuki Drop system. Cut three lengths of the lumber, each 8' and 2" long.

Lined up together, the three lengths of lumber will form a 24' 6" long backboard. The backboard should be slightly longer than the width of the curtain you are dropping.

Flat Braces

6 x flat braces about 3" x 2" in size are used to connect the three lengths of lumber together to form the backboard.

You can also cut out lengths of 2" aluminum flat bar (3mm thick) to use as the connectors.

Bolts with Washers and Hex Nuts

4 x 1.75" Bolts (8mm in diameter) with Washers and Hex Nuts will secure the connectors to the lumber.

Angle Braces

4" x 4" angle braces will be used as support hooks to attach the backboard to the flying bar. You will need four pieces.

Eye Screws (8mm thick)

28 x ¾" long eye screws are needed in all. 18 eye screws will form 9 pairs of "loops" for the Kabuki Drop system. 10 eye screws will acts as guides for the Pull Cord.

"PINS & LOOPS" DROP

Eye Bolts (8mm thick).

You will need 8 x 2" long eye bolts that will act as the "pins" for the Kabuki Drop system. These are similar to eye screws but without a pointed end and finer threads. Look for eye bolts with a forged head and not a wired head.

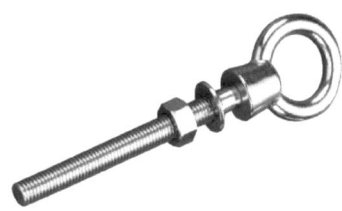

While not a necessity, it is preferable to smoothen out the threads on the eye bolts to reduce friction.

There are 3 ways to do this:

1. If you can find them at the right length, threadless eye bolts will be ideal but are not always available at regular hardware stores, even large ones.

2. Alternatively, you can also use a grinder to grind the threads smooth. However, this is a professional tool that may not be readily available.

3. An easier solution is to buy PVC flexible tubing, fit it snugly over the threaded shaft of the eye bolts and trim to length.

Steel Wire 1.5mm thick with Ferrules

Ferrules are "collars" made of aluminum that are fitted over wires and crimped down with pliers to form a strong lock on two ends or lengths of wire.

Ferrules will be available at all hardware stores that sell the steel wire and come in specific sizes to fit the diameter of the wire.

Rope

Braided polypropylene nylon rope with a core, 7mm thick, is used as the Pull Cord. A 24ft wide curtain in a regular theatre venue will require a Pull Cord of about 30ft long.

Pulley

The pulley should have a loop head attachment and should be large enough to accommodate the thickness of the pull cord.

Heavy Duty Cable Ties

8mm wide cable ties will be used to secure the backboard to the flying bar.

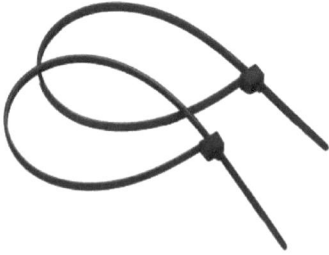

Curtain

The curtain is prepared with grommets attached along the top or attached to a header with grommets as described in "Basic

Components of the Manual Kabuki Drop". 1.5" stainless steel split rings are attached to each grommet.

Always make the curtain only after you have made the system.

HOW TO BUILD THE SYSTEM

Step 1 - Backboard

Drill a pair of 8mm holes at each corner of each length of lumber. Then drill one more pair of holes in the center of each length of lumber. These holes are the cable ties that will secure the backboard to the flying bar.

Next, lay the three lengths of lumber out in a straight line to form the entire backboard of the Kabuki Drop system. It should measure 24' 6" long.

Use the pieces of flat brace as connectors to connect all three lengths of lumber together. There will be one connector each on the back and front of the lumber.

Drill 8mm holes through the connectors and the lumber. Thread the four 1.75" bolts through the connectors & lumber and secure them in place with the washers and hex nuts. See Fig 1.

FIG 1

FRONT VIEW

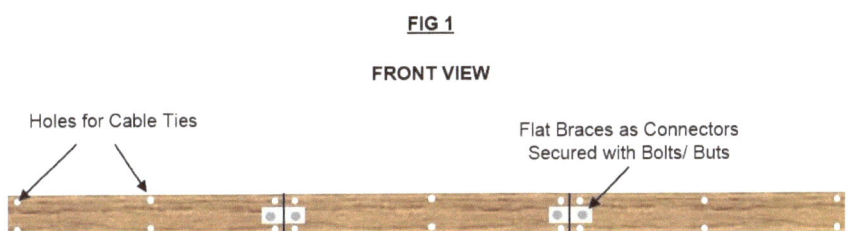

"PINS & LOOPS" DROP

Step 2 – Backboard Support Hooks

Using wood screws, screw down one end of an angle brace to the top of the backboard. There should be one at each corner and two evenly spaced out in middle length of the backboard.

This will give you four support hooks that will allow you to hang the backboard onto the flying bar. See Figs 2 & 3 below.

Step 3 - "Loops"

The "loops" or drop points consist of eye screws that are screwed into the backboard in pairs, near the bottom edge. Each pair of eye screws are positioned about 1" apart from each other.

Each pair is set about 3ft from each other for the length of the backboard. These eye screws will act as the holders for the pins that will hold up the curtain.

Another set of eye screws are the guides for the pull cord and are positioned 1" in from each top corner of the backboard as well as between each pair of "loops". See Figs 2 & 3.

FIG 2

FRONT VIEW

(Only 4ft length of the Backboard is shown)

Angle Brace as Support Hook

Eye Screws as Guides for Pull Cord

Backboard

Eye Screws as "Loops" for Kabuki Drop System

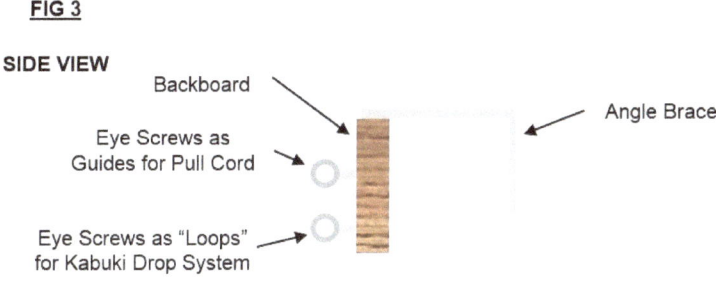

Step 4 - "Pins"

Attach a length of steel wire to each eye bolt and forms loops using the ferrules to secure the loops in place. The finished length of wire should be 2.5" long and the free loop should be large enough to thread the pull cord through. See Fig 4.

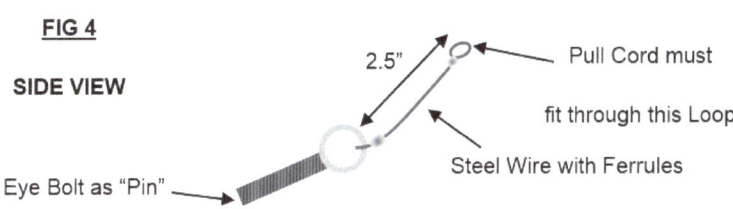

SET-UP

For purposes of instruction, we will assume the pull cord will be pulled to the stage left side to activate the curtain drop.

Step 1 – Securing the Backboard to the Flying Bars

Lower the flying bar to a comfortable height at stage level.

If you are working with a fixed horizontal that cannot be lowered, you will need to use a scissors lift, scaffolding or ladder.

Hook the backboard onto the flying bar using the support hooks. Next, secure the backboard to the flying bar with the heavy duty cable ties through the drilled holes in the backboard. See Fig 5.

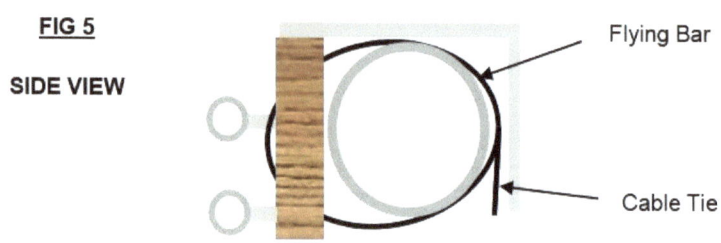

FIG 5

SIDE VIEW

Flying Bar

Cable Tie

Step 2 – Setting Up the Pull Cord

Insert all the "pins" (eye bolts) into each pair of "loops" (eye screws).

Thread one end of the pull cord through the very first eyelet (pull cord guide) near the top corner of the backboard. This will be the side closest to stage right.

Tie a large knot (knots over knots) or "Monkey Fist" knot at the end of the pull cord. The knot should be large enough so it cannot fit through the eyelet. In essence, this first eye screw will act as a stopper so that the pull cord does not get pulled through the eye screw.

Ensure there is about 4" of cord between the knot and the eye screw.

Thread the pull cord through the steel wire loop of the first "pin". Tie a knot over the steel wire loop. Ensure the rope ends up towards stage left and is not twisted.

You want the knot to be in a position such that the steel wire is stretched out away from the head of the "pin".

Thread the pull cord through the next pull cord guide and then through the steel wire of the second "pin". Tie another knot over the steel wire loop and continue for the rest of the pins till the end of backboard. See Fig 6.

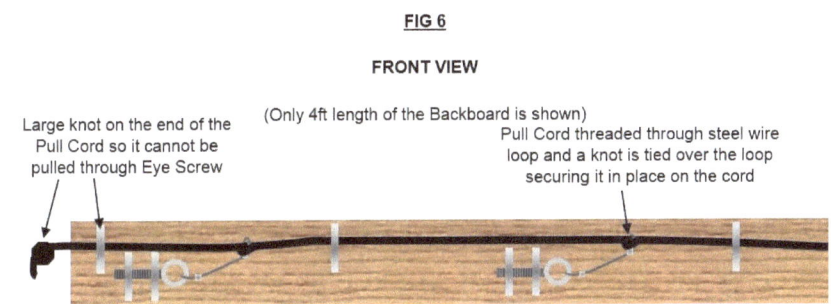

FIG 6

FRONT VIEW

(Only 4ft length of the Backboard is shown)

Large knot on the end of the Pull Cord so it cannot be pulled through Eye Screw

Pull Cord threaded through steel wire loop and a knot is tied over the loop securing it in place on the cord

Step 3 – Setting Up Pulley

The pulley is attached to the end of the flying bar with a cable tie so that the pull cord hangs down at the side of the stage.

If everything is set up correctly, when the pull cord is tugged, all the "pins" will be pulled free from the "loops".

The pull cord guides and the steel wires attached to the "pins", will ensure the "pins" and pull cord will remain attached to the backboard after the pins have been pulled out. See Fig 7.

"PINS & LOOPS" DROP

FIG 7
FRONT VIEW

(Only 4ft length of the Backboard is shown)

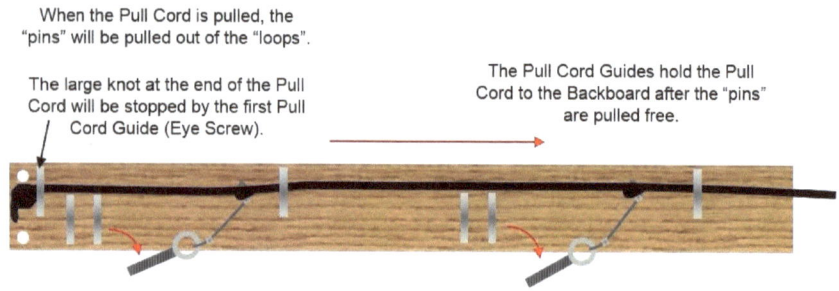

When the Pull Cord is pulled, the "pins" will be pulled out of the "loops".

The large knot at the end of the Pull Cord will be stopped by the first Pull Cord Guide (Eye Screw).

The Pull Cord Guides hold the Pull Cord to the Backboard after the "pins" are pulled free.

CURTAIN SET-UP & DROP

Step 1 – Attaching the Curtain to the Backboard

Replace all the "pins" into the "loops" (eye screws) but first place the split rings attached to the grommets in the top of the curtain between each pair of eye screws. This will attach the curtain to the drop points.

Step 2 – Raising the Flying Bar

Raise the flying bar up so that the curtain is fully stretched out covering the stage.

Gently keep the pull cord relatively taut and secure the free end to a weight, side lighting truss or tie it to a chair.

Step 3 – Dropping the Curtain

To drop the curtain, simply pull the pull cord to disengage all the "pins". The split rings will slip off the "pins" and the curtain will fall to the floor.

ALTERNATIVE METAL CONSTRUCTION

If you like and are comfortable working with metal, you can build an all-metal version of the Kabuki Drop. It has a more professional look, faster installation time, is lighter in weight and will last a lifetime if used in normal conditions.

Instead of the lumber, the backboard can be made from **Aluminum Rectangle Tubing** 2" x 1" (3mm thick). This is pre-fabricated extruded aluminum that you can buy off the shelf.

All the eye screws will be replaced with **Eye Bolts** that bolt through the aluminum rectangle tubing.

Instead of the support hooks and cable ties that are needed to secure the backboard to the flying bar, you can use **Lighting G-Clamps**.

This a clamp used for stage lighting that can be clamped and screwed tight into the flying bar. You will have to replace the bolt that usually is bolted to the stage lighting fixture to a longer bolt measuring 3" long.

"PINS & LOOPS" DROP

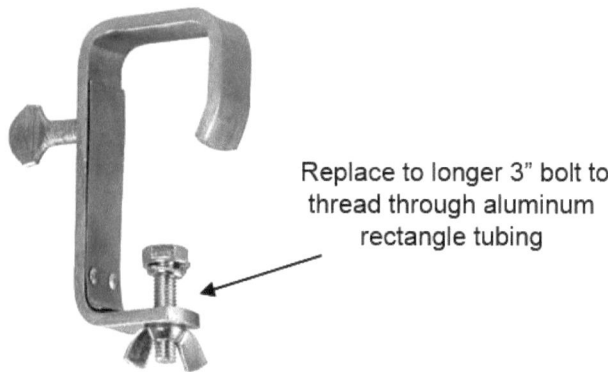

Replace to longer 3" bolt to thread through aluminum rectangle tubing

Drill holes through the aluminum tubing from the top to bottom of the tubing (through the 1" side of the tubing). Two clamps should be used for every 8ft length of aluminum tubing.

Ensure that the bolts for the G-Clamps do not interfere with the eyelet bolts used for as the "loops" and the pull cord guides.

All other aspects of the system remain the same.

"PULL BACK" DROP

This is called the "Pull Back" Kabuki Drop as the method requires the system to be physically pulled back with a pull cord.

While the concept is similar to the traditional "rolling pole" method, the pole is replaced by a rectangular lumber (wood) backboard that is tipped back (and forward) instead of rotating like the pole.

Bolts that are attached through the backboard act as the pegs for the Kabuki curtain to be hung on.

Lengths of aluminum flat bar are bent to form brackets that are secured over a theatre flying or lighting bar and bolted to the backboard. These brackets hang securely but loosely on the flying bar so that the backboard is able to rock back and forth on the flying bar.

A pull cord is attached to the bottom of the backboard via an eye screw and runs to the back of the top of the stage, over the last flying bar and down to the floor.

"PULL BACK" DROP

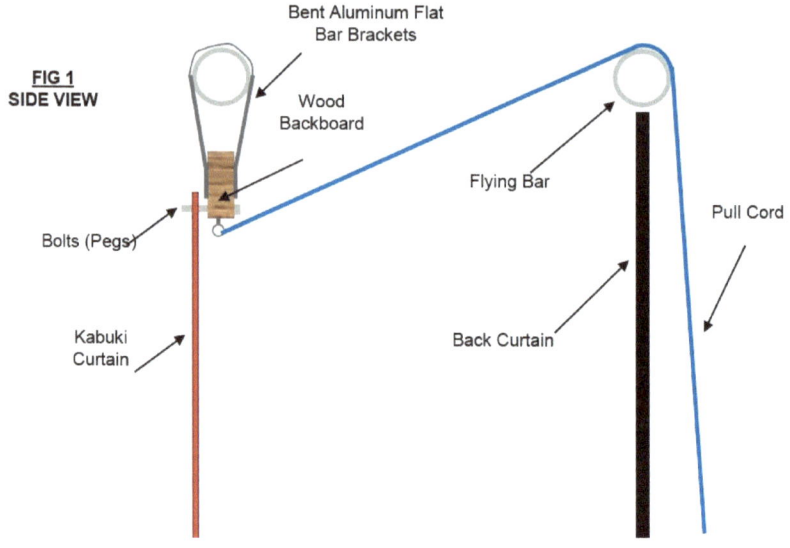

When the pull cord is pulled down, the backboard will be tipped back (and forward), allowing the curtain to fall off the pegs (bolts) and onto the floor.

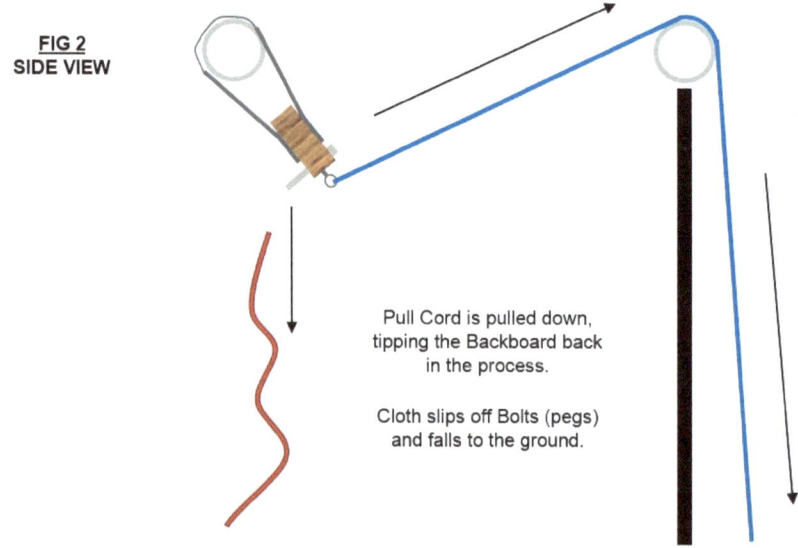

WHAT YOU NEED

You will need the following materials to build this system (based on a 24ft wide curtain):

1" x 2" Lumber

This will form the backboard of the Kabuki Drop system. Cut three lengths of the lumber, each 8' and 2" long.

Lined up together, the three lengths of lumber will form a 24' 6" long backboard.

The backboard should be slightly longer than the width of the curtain you are dropping.

Bolts with Washers and Hex Nuts

You will need:

- 13 x 3" Bolts (6mm in diameter) with Washers and Hex Nuts that will act as the drop points for the curtain.

- 8 x 1.75" Bolts (8mm in diameter) with Washers and Hex Nuts to secure the brackets and connectors to the lumber.

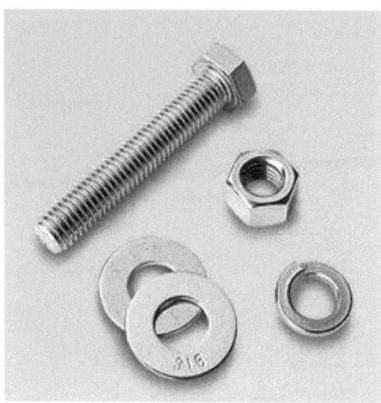

1" Aluminum Flat Bar (2mm thick)

Cut four lengths of the aluminum flat bar, 24" long each. These will be made into hanging brackets that will secure the backboard to the flying bar.

You will also need four more short lengths that will act as connectors to connect the three lengths of backboard to form one long backboard. Cut four lengths of the aluminum flat bar, 4" long each.

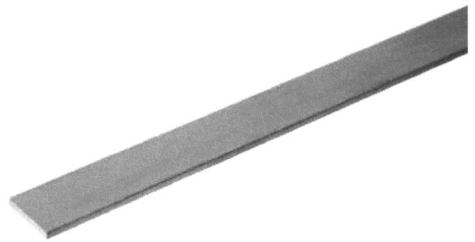

1 x 1.25" Eye Screw (8mm)

This will be mounted on the bottom of the backboard and act as the pull cord attachment.

Rope

Braided polypropylene nylon rope with a core, 7mm thick, is used as the Pull Cord. A 24ft wide curtain in a regular theatre venue will require a Pull Cord of about 30ft long.

Curtain

The curtain is prepared with grommets attached across the top edge of the fabric, each about 2ft apart from each other.

Always make the curtain only after you have made the system.

HOW TO MAKE THE SYSTEM

Step 1 - Backboard

Lay the three lengths of lumber out in a straight line to form the entire backboard of the Kabuki Drop system. It should measure 24' 6" long.

"PULL BACK" DROP

The four 4" lengths of 1" aluminum flat bar will be used as connectors to connect all three lengths of lumber together. There will be one connector each on the back and front of the lumber.

Drill 8mm holes through the connectors and the lumber. Thread four 1.75" bolts through the connectors & lumber and secure them in place with the washers and hex nuts.

Step 2 – "Pegs"

Drill 13 x 6mm diameter holes through the lumber in a straight row as shown in Fig 3. These holes are for the 3" bolts that will act as drop points or pegs for the Kabuki Drop system. Insert the 3" bolts through the holes and secure them in place with the washers and hex nuts.

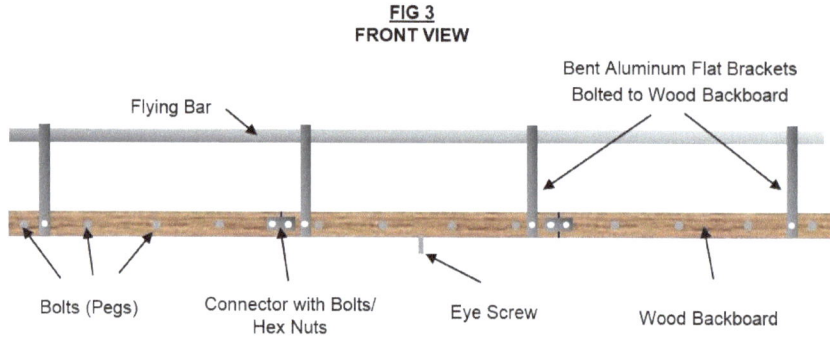

FIG 3
FRONT VIEW

Step 3 - Brackets

Form each 24" length of 1" aluminum flat bar into a bracket as shown in Fig 4.

One way of doing this is to take one end of the aluminum flat bar and clamp it in a vice. Use a 2.5 pole as a form and fold/ bend the aluminum flat bar over it. The idea is to get a rounded bend about 2.5" in diameter in the middle of the flat bar.

Repeat for the other 3 lengths of flat bar. Use the remaining 4 x 1.75" bolt/ nut sets to secure the brackets to the backboard.

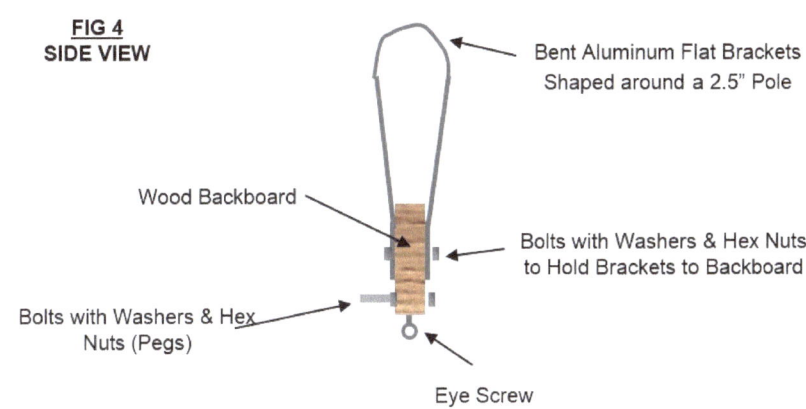

Step 4 – Pull Cord Attachment

Drill a 6mm hole about ¾" deep under the backboard, centered. Screw in the eye screw tightly.

CURTAIN SET-UP & DROP

Step 1 – Securing the Backboard to the Flying Bars

Lower the flying bar that you wish to mount the Kabuki Drop onto to a comfortable height at stage level.

If you are working with a fixed horizontal that cannot be lowered, you will need to use a scissors lift, scaffolding or ladder.

Secure the backboard to the flying bar in the following way: You will have to remove the hex nut from the bolt that holds the bracket to the backboard. Carefully lift off that end of the bracket from the end of the bolt but ensure the bolt remains threaded through the backboard.

Hook the free end of the bracket over the flying bar and thread it back onto the end of the bolt. Screw the hex nut back onto the bolt tightly.

Repeat for the rest of the brackets.

The Kabuki Drop system will be securely mounted onto the flying bar but due to the design of the brackets, will also be able to rock back and forth as needed.

Step 2 – Attaching the Curtain to the Backboard

Take the curtain and hook the grommets onto the pegs of the backboard so that the entire curtain is stretched out across the backboard.

Step 3 – Setting up the Pull Cord

Raise the flying bar closest to the back of the stage (upstage) down to stage level. This will likely be the flying bar that holds the back curtain of the stage.

If there are flying or lighting bars between the flying bar that you mounted the Kabuki Drop system on and the most upstage flying bar, you will have to lower them as well.

Tie one end of your pull cord securely to the eye screw under the backboard. Guide the free end of the pull cord over all the flying/lighting bars so that it drops over and behind the back curtain.

Step 4 – Setting up the Drop

Raise up the flying bars but gently pull and guide the pull cord from behind the back curtain ensuring it does not get knotted or tangled.

The Kabuki Drop should be set up as shown in Fig 1.

Step 5 – Dropping the Curtain

To drop the curtain, simply pull the pull cord to tip the backboard back enough so that the curtain slips off the pegs and falls to the floor. See Fig 2.

"ROLL & DROP" DROP

This is a modern design for the traditional "rolling pole" Japanese Kabuki Drop but updated with modern materials and trigger mechanism.

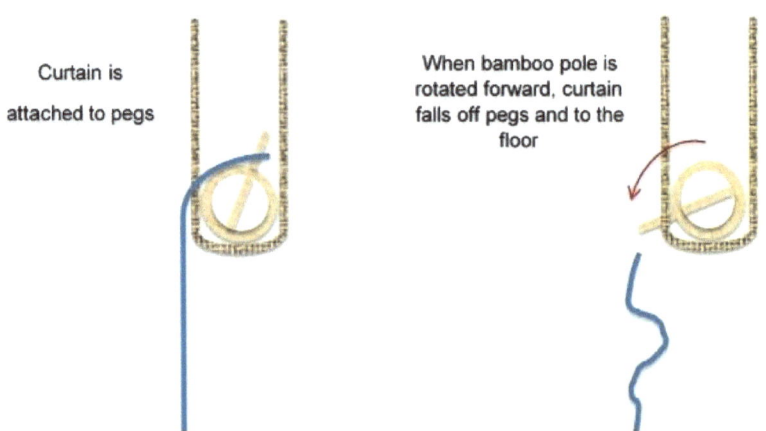

It is made completely with metal and is relatively lightweight. It is very reliable as there is only one connection point that needs to be released in order to effect the curtain drop.

WHAT YOU NEED

You will need the following materials to build this system (based on a 24ft wide curtain):

Aluminum Round Tubing 1.5" (3mm thick)

This is pre-fabricated extruded aluminum that you can buy off the shelf. It should be 6" longer than the width of the curtain you are dropping.

The total length you will require is 24' 6". I suggest cutting three lengths measuring 8' 2" long each.

Use the connectors suggested in the "World's Easiest" Drop to connect the three lengths of tubing to form one long pole.

FIG 1

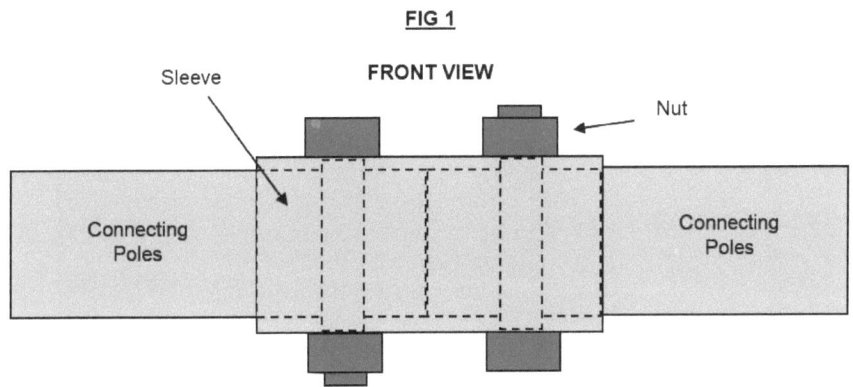

Bolts (6mm thick) with Washers & Hex Lock-Nuts

You will need 13 sets of 4" long bolts with washers and hex lock-nuts. A lock-nut is a nut with a plastic thread that "locks" the nut in place when it is screwed onto the bolt.

The bolt sets will act as drop points or "pegs" for the Kabuki Drop.

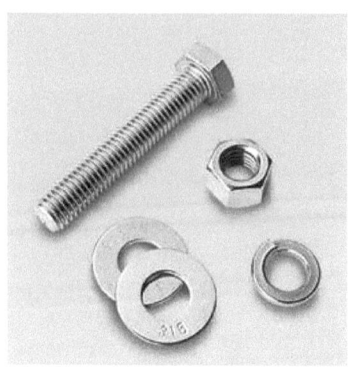

Eye Bolt (8mm thick)

You will need one eye bolt. The length will depend on your set-up as explained below.

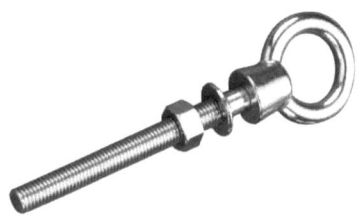

Pipe Mounting Brackets

This piece of hardware comes in many different designs and attachment methods. You want a pipe clamp that can adjust to accommodate a 1.5" diameter pipe.

It should also have a connection point or hole that allows for a threaded bolt to be screwed into/ through it. You will need 4 pieces.

The pipe mounting bracket is shown on the left below.

Lighting G-Clamps

This a clamp used for stage lighting that can be clamped and screwed tight into the flying bar. The bolt usually meant to be secured to a stage lighting fixture will be screwed into the pipe mounting bracket. You will need 4 pieces.

Together, the pipe mounting bracket and the G-Clamp will form the pipe clamp assembly. A total of 4 sets.

 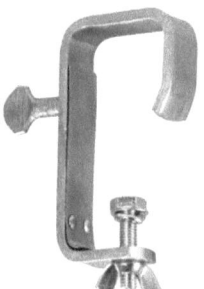

Spring Latch

Ideally, you want one that has an eye bolt or ring at the end and has a mounting plate so that you can secure it to the flying bar.

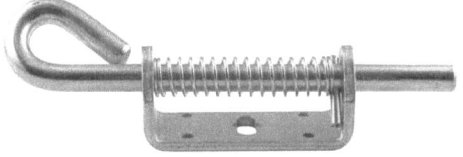

Rope

Braided polypropylene nylon rope with a core, 7mm thick, is used as the Pull Cord. A 24ft wide curtain in a regular theatre venue will require a Pull Cord of about 30ft long.

Pulley

The pulley should have a loop head attachment and should be large enough to accommodate the thickness of the pull cord.

Heavy Duty Cable Ties

8mm wide cable ties will be used to secure the spring latch and pull cord to the flying bar.

Curtain

The curtain is prepared with grommets, every 2ft, along the top or attached to a header with grommets as described in "Basic Components of the Manual Kabuki Drop". There is no need for split rings on the grommets for this system.

Always make the curtain only after you have made the system.

HOW TO MAKE THE SYSTEM

Step 1 – Drop Points

The drop points consist of multiple bolts ("pegs") protruding out along the length of the aluminum round tubing.

Drill 6mm diameter holes through both sides of the tubing and thread the 4" long bolts through the holes.

The bolts at each end are set 3" in from each end of the tubing. Each subsequent bolt is set approximately 3ft apart from each other.

Secure the bolts with washers and lock-nuts. See Fig 1.

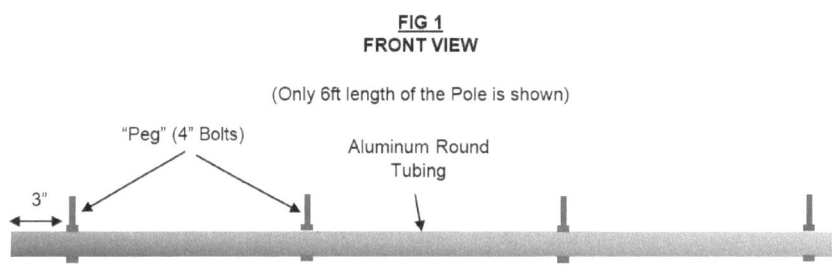

**FIG 1
FRONT VIEW**

(Only 6ft length of the Pole is shown)

"Peg" (4" Bolts)

Aluminum Round Tubing

3"

Step 2 – Release Mechanism Attachment

You will now need to attach an 8mm eye bolt that will act as a connection point for the rolling bar. However, you can only determine the length of the eye bolt only after you set up the system to the flying bar.

However, for now, you need to determine the position of the holes and drill the necessary holes first.

The eye bolt needs to be threaded through the middle of the length of tubing. However, the angle of the holes will be about 45 degrees away from angle of the protruding "pegs".

Mark out the position of the eye bolt on the tubing and drill holes through both sides of the tubing, ensuring the holes line up perfectly straight.

Eventually, you will thread the eye bolt through and use two lock nuts to secure the eye bolt in place. One lock nut is positioned on either side of the tubing so that the "eye" of the eye bolt protrudes out as shown in Fig 2.

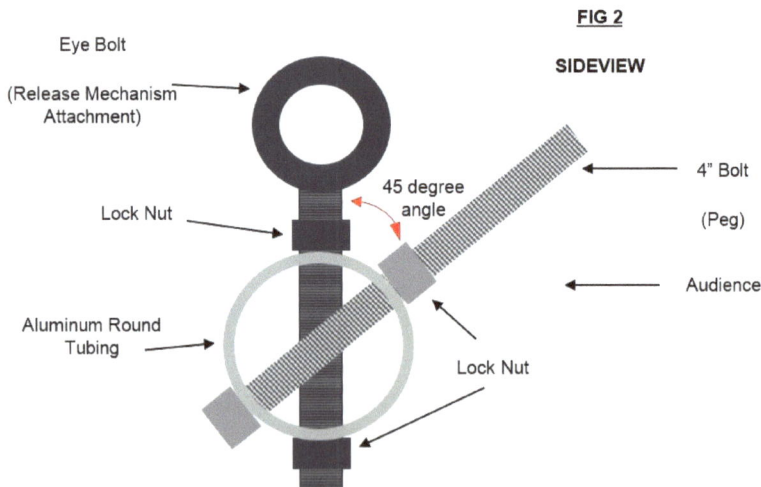

Step 3 – Pipe Clamp Assembly

The aluminum round tubing will be held by pipe clamps assembly as described above. You will need a pipe clamp assembly for about every 8ft length of tubing. So for this 24' 6" pole, you will need a total of 4 sets.

The pipe clamps are loosened as necessary so that the pole can freely rotate within the clamps.

FIRST-TIME SET- UP

For purposes of instruction, we will assume the pull cord will be pulled to the stage left side to activate the curtain drop.

Step 1 – Securing the Rolling Pole to the Flying Bar

Lower the flying bar to a comfortable height at stage level.

If you are working with a fixed horizontal support that cannot be lowered, you will need to use a scissors lift, scaffolding or ladder.

Attach the pipe clamp assemblies onto the flying bar via the lighting G-Clamps but do not tighten the bolts so they can be repositioned.

Open up the pipe mounting brackets as necessary and insert the pole into them. Ensure the pipe clamps at the very ends are on the outside of the end "pegs".

Once the pole is in the right position, you can tighten both the pipe mounting brackets and the G-Clamps.

Step 2 – Setting Up of Release Mechanism & Connection

Take the spring latch and secure it (upside down) underneath the flying bar with cable ties. Alternatively, you could mount the spring latch to a piece of wood that is also attached to G-Clamps that you secure to the flying bar.

Regardless of how you mount the spring latch, it should be positioned just above the center of the pole held underneath it.

This will determine the length of eye bolt that you require. It has to be long enough for the spring latch to be inserted through it.

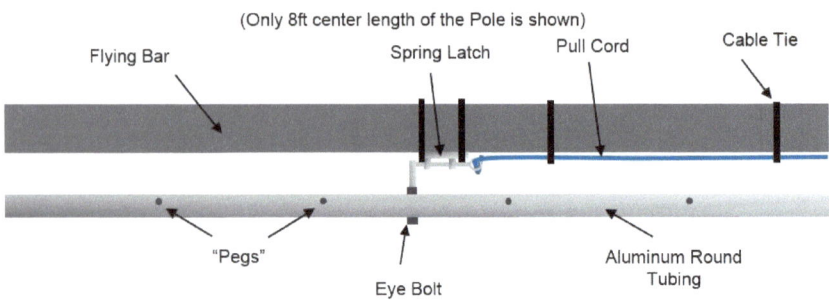

FIG 3

FRONT VIEW

Assuming the distance between the top of the pole and the spring latch is 6", you will need an eye bolt about 8" long. This is so that there is enough length to thread the bolt through the 1.5" pole and screw a lock nut at the end.

Once you attach the eye bolt, adjust the position of the spring latch as necessary so that it can be inserted through the eye bolt and hold the pole securely in position.

Step 3 – Setting Up of the Pull Cord

Tie one end of the pull cord to the spring latch. This is where the eye bolt on the spring latch will come in handy. Tie the pull rope securely and use electric tape to and tape up the end to the main body of the rope.

You will now "lay" the pull cord upside down along the flying bar towards stage left in the following way:

Tie cable ties loosely around the flying bar from the spring latch to the stage left end of the flying bar, about 2ft apart from each other.

Thread the free end of the pull cord through this loose cable ties that will act as guides so that the pull cord will be held close to the flying bar. Refer back to Fig 3.

Step 4 – Setting Up of the Pulley

The pulley is attached to the end of the flying bar with a cable tie so that the pull cord hangs down at the side of the stage.

If everything is set up correctly, when the pull cord is tugged, the spring latch will be pulled back from the eye bolt. This will release the pole causing it to rotate forward due to gravity.

CURTAIN SET-UP & DROP

Reset the pole and reset the spring latch to hold the tubing in the "set-up" position.

Attach the curtain to the drop points by hanging the grommets over the "pegs".

Raise the flying bar up so that the curtain is fully stretched out covering the stage.

Gently keep the pull cord relatively taut and secure the free end to a weight, side lighting truss or tie it to a chair.

To drop the curtain, simply pull the pull cord to pull back the spring latch. The tubing will rotate forward and the curtain will slip off the "pegs" and fall to the floor.

The **Pro Magic Kabuki Drop System** is a handmade custom-machined professional manual curtain drop system that packs small, is lightweight, highly flexible and 100% dependable.

Best of all, the system is very inexpensive - a fraction of the price of electronic systems!

The Pro Magic Kabuki Drop is a strap-on system for medium to large curtain drops (full theatre proscenium) and is secured on flying bars, lighting truss or almost any horizontal support structure.

Check out these amazing features:

- Easy to Use
- Lightweight, Compact & Durable
- Fast Set-up/ Almost Instant Reset/ Very Short Tear-Down Time
- Silent & Dependable
- Low Cost
- Completely Self-Contained

The highly flexible system was designed for:

- Theatre Productions
- Concerts
- Stage Shows
- Performing Artistes' Acts
- Corporate & Special Events

Available as a SINGLE and DOUBLE Kabuki Drop.

If you are looking for an affordable professional Kabuki Drop system, this is the perfect solution!

For specifications and to watch the demo video, visit:

MagicKabukiDrop.com/shop

www.ingramcontent.com/pod-product-compliance
Lightning Source LLC
Chambersburg PA
CBHW041609220426
43667CB00001B/15